The Ultimate OFFICIAL Guide to

Disney
CLUB PENGUIN ™

VOLUME 1

By Katherine Noll

Published by Ladybird Books Ltd 2009
A Penguin Company

Penguin Books Ltd, 80 Strand,
London, WC2R ORL, UK
Penguin Books Australia Ltd,
Camberwell, Victoria, Australia
Penguin Group (NZ), 67 Apollo Drive, Rosedale, North Shore
0632, New Zealand
(a division of Pearson New Zealand Ltd)

www.ladybird.com

ISBN: 9781409302711

10 9 8 7 6 5 4 3 2

Printed in Slovakia

Hello, Penguins!

The Club Penguin team is always hard at work creating new and exciting stuff. Over the years we've designed games, parties, characters, clothes, items, and more—the list is huge!

That's why we created this guidebook. It's packed with tons of wacky, wonderful facts and memories. And because it's all contained neatly between two book covers, you can dive into Club Penguin even when you're not plugged into the Internet.

On these pages you'll read about all the things you can do on Club Penguin:
- Make friends
- Play games
- Explore rooms and places all over the island
- Adopt a pet called a puffle
- Go to parties held on holidays and special occasions
- Take part in scavenger hunts and contests

There's lots more things to do, too. So turn the page, check it out, and when you're done, log in to Club Penguin, and let us know what you think. We always love to hear what you have to say!

Waddle on!

The Club Penguin Team
Posted by Billybob

Table of Contents

Getting Started

Whether you've just arrived on the island or you're a seasoned expert, there are always new things to discover. This book is your guide to the ultimate Club Penguin experience.

How to Use This Book

- Read it from cover to cover to become a Club Penguin expert
- Skip to the sections you're most interested in
- Share what you learn here with other penguins
- Get ideas for new things you can do with your buddies
- Read the game tips and secrets to become a master gamer
- Keep a written record of your Club Penguin experience

How NOT to Use This Book

- As kindling for your bonfire
- As a snack for your puffle
- For snowball target practice
- As a doorstop
- As a flyswatter
- As a flotation device in a water landing
- As a sled

Look for These Penguins as You Read

AUNT ARCTIC SAYS

Hello! My name is Aunt Arctic.

I write a column for *The Club Penguin Times*. In this guide, I'll be sharing interesting facts, tips, and secrets with you.

I'm a Club Penguin Tour Guide.

I'll be introducing you to the different sections of this book—and the different areas of Club Penguin.

Safety First

Before we get too far in, let's review some important points on safety. Club Penguin takes many steps to ensure everyone can stay safe while they're playing on the island, but there are a few basic safety rules everyone should know before diving into the Internet.

- **Keep personal information to yourself.** Never share it online! That includes your real name, age, address, location, phone number, or school.

- **Keep your password safe and private.** Never share it with anyone but your parent or guardian. If someone else gets it, they might pretend to be you. They could give out personal information or get you into trouble.

- **Tell a parent if someone says or does something on the Internet that makes you feel uncomfortable.** Also tell them if someone asks you for personal information.

- **Only visit websites that are monitored by moderators.** On Club Penguin the [M] symbol on the right of the screen means the site is moderated every day. Moderators are committed to making sure Club Penguin is safe. Other penguins online help keep Club Penguin safe, too.

- **Report players who break the rules to a moderator.** Penguins found using inappropriate language will be banned. If a penguin says or does something inappropriate, you can report them to a moderator. Click the penguin and their player card will appear. Choose the [M] to make a report.

Club Penguin Rules

1. Always have fun!

2. Help other penguins who ask.

3. Use appropriate language. Do not swear or use other bad language.

4. Safety first. Do not ask another penguin for personal information such as their real name or phone number.

5. Respect other penguins. Do not act in any way that is mean or rude.

6. Do not ask anyone for his or her password.

If you break any of the rules, you risk being banned from Club Penguin. This means you will not be able to use your account for a period of time. Sometimes it's for twenty-four hours or it could be forever.

Creating Your Penguin

Do you love sports? Would you rather dance and listen to music? Or would you prefer to sit home and read a good book? Maybe you like to do all of those things! Every penguin has a different personality. On Club Penguin, you can customize yourself to show off the things that make you uniquely you.

Your personality starts with a name, but it doesn't end there. You can choose a color to match your mood. You can choose a background for your player card that shows off your interests. If you have a membership, you can buy clothes and accessories.

But showing off your personality isn't just about how you look—it's about what you *do*. You can let other penguins know what kind of penguin you are by the way you greet other penguins, by challenging them to a Sled Race, by dancing when you're happy, or by helping out a lost penguin when you see one.

If you're not sure how to shape your penguin identity, don't sweat it. Pick something and try it out. You can always change your mind! That's the great thing about Club Penguin. If you get a haircut you don't like, for example, you can get rid of it with a click, instead of waiting for weeks for it to grow out.

Your Name

Anyone who has been on Club Penguin for a while knows how important choosing a penguin name is—once you choose it there's no going back! Finding the right name isn't always easy, but with a bit of imagination anything is possible. If a friend asks you for help choosing a name, try these suggestions.

1. **Never use your real name!** Club Penguin is a safe place online for friends to interact. One of the best ways to stay safe is to never give out your real name on the Internet.

2. **Use your imagination.** Try a made-up name. One penguin we know is named Mcsugarface, for example.

3. **Think of your favorite things**. Use your favorite color, animal, or sports team as part of your name.

4. **Try two.** Combine two of your favorite things into one name. For example: banana + burger = Bananaburger.

5. **Add some numbers.** If the name you want is taken, add some numbers to it to make it different. For safety reasons, don't use your birthday or address. Make sure your name is between four characters and twelve characters long.

Once you come up with your name, write it down, along with your password. Give this to a parent and ask them to keep it safe for you, in case you forget.

Check Out the Home Page

I enjoy clicking on different things on the home page. You can click on the yellow puffle to see it paint. Click on the starfish on the ground and watch it change into other objects. And see that blue phone next to the Lighthouse? If you click on it, a mysterious penguin in sunglasses will appear. You'll learn more about this kind of penguin in the section of this book called "Hidden Places."

Be sure to explore the home page at clubpenguin.com before you dive in and play. There are a lot of helpful features to check out on the website before you get into the game.

Watch a Video. Click on the blue penguin to see a special presentation of everything Club Penguin offers.

Read the What's New blog. It's located in the Community section of the website; click the orange or yellow penguin on the home page to find the blog. It's updated every week and is a quick way to find out about upcoming parties, special events, new games, catalog releases, and even some insider info you won't find anywhere else. Be sure to post a comment and let everyone know what you think! Billybob, the main author of the blog, loves to hear from other penguins.

Find Answers to Questions. Click on the word *help* on the top of the screen to be taken to a list of tutorials. They will show you how to do everything from walking around to playing games. You can also get help here with the technical problems you're having.

Using Your Toolbar

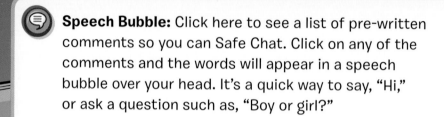

Speech Bubble: Click here to see a list of pre-written comments so you can Safe Chat. Click on any of the comments and the words will appear in a speech bubble over your head. It's a quick way to say, "Hi," or ask a question such as, "Boy or girl?"

Winking Face: Click here for a list of emotes you can use—little icons that show how you're feeling without using words.

Blue Penguin: Click here for a list of motions you can make: dance, wave, or sit.

Snowball: Click on the snowball to throw a snowball. A round circle will appear on your screen after you click. Move the circle to the place you want your snowball to land. Then click.

Speech Bar: Use this bar to type in your own messages if you are not in Ultimate Safe Chat. When you are done typing, press the speech bubble to the right of the bar. The message will appear in a bubble over you.

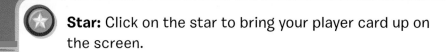 **Star:** Click on the star to bring your player card up on the screen.

Smiley Face: Click on this to see a list of your buddies. You can click on a buddy's name at any time to see their player card. If a buddy is online, you will see a yellow face next to your buddy's name.

House: Click on this to enter your igloo.

Question Mark: Click on the question mark to get to your account settings. You can change your password, cancel your membership, or activate Ultimate Safe Chat. You can also find out how old you are.

What Does it Mean to Have a Membership?

It doesn't cost any money to join Club Penguin. But a parent can sign you up for a membership and pay a monthly fee. Players with a membership get to do special things on Club Penguin, such as buy clothes or furniture for their igloos. When you see this symbol in the book , it means the activity is for players with a membership only.

TOURS

Ready to Dive In?

Once you're up to speed, go ahead and log in. You will usually be dropped in the Town Center, unless the server you're in is very crowded. Then you might find yourself in the Plaza, the Ski Village, or some other spot. You can use your mouse to move around. Follow the paths to get to different places. Or click on the [MAP] on the lower left of your screen. Then click on the place you want to visit, and you will be transported there.

If you want to go right to your igloo, click on the icon on the toolbar on the bottom of your screen. To leave your igloo, walk to the door, and the map will appear. (You can also just click on the map in the lower left corner.)

Before you start to explore, you might want to read the newspaper. It's on the upper left part of your screen. A new issue of the newspaper comes out every Thursday. Next to the What's New blog, it's the best way to find out what's happening on Club Penguin. Every issue has special tips and advice from a Tour Guide as well as Aunt Arctic.

If you haven't taken the plunge yet, this is a good time to start exploring Club Penguin. Don't be afraid to visit new places. Click on things to find out what they do. And if you have questions, ask other penguins to help you.

TIP

Back issues of the newspaper are stored in file cabinets in the Boiler Room. You can get into the Boiler Room by entering the Night Club and walking up to the fourth speaker to the right of the door.

Town Center

"Let's begin our tour of Club Penguin in the central hub of the island. Town Center is always crowded with penguins. If you want to make an announcement, ask around about the new hidden pin, or invite penguins to your party, this is the place to go.

"Town Center is a great place to penguin-watch. Take a seat in front of the Coffee Shop and see who passes by. You might see a parade of penguins in colorful costumes, groups of penguins dressed alike, or penguins playing tag or having snowball fights. If you see something that looks like fun, join in!

"You'll also find the Coffee Shop, the Night Club, or the Gift Shop at the Town Center. There's plenty to do in these places, whether you're in the mood to shop, play a game, read, or make new friends."

First Stop: COFFEE SHOP

Town Center is always buzzing with news and information, and you'll find the same atmosphere inside the Coffee Shop. Take a seat on one of the comfy red couches. You may see a server in an apron working, ready to pour you a hot, tasty beverage. Drink a cup while you read the newspaper and catch up with what's new.

Want to earn some coins while you're there? Waddle over to the bags of java and play *Bean Counters*, where you unload bags of coffee beans from a delivery truck. There's always work to be done on Club Penguin, so if you and a friend are looking for a quiet place to kick back away from the crowds, head upstairs to the Book Room.

Book Room

As soon as you enter you'll hear the strains of a reggae beat, setting a funky vibe for this room. In here you'll find an abstract painting on the wall, strange sculptures, and a shelf overflowing with books. Tables scattered around the room hold a game called *mancala*, a popular activity among strategy-minded penguins.

You'll often see penguins clustered together in conversation. Penguins have been known to give freestyle poetry performances here, inspired by the artistic space. If you feel like reading, check out the bookshelf to find everything from storybooks to the Club Penguin yearbook, which is a review of events over the years. Or play *Paint By Letters*, where you get to help a story become illustrated—and earn coins while you're doing it.

TIP

In the Book Room, read the book *Rockhopper and the Stowaway*. You will find the free item on the last page.

AUNT ARCTIC SAYS

Penguins often ask me how they, too, can become servers at the Coffee Shop. The key to being a server is the green apron. If you have a Club Penguin membership, you can purchase the apron in the Gift Shop. To perform the pouring coffee action, you must be wearing the apron and nothing else— not even shoes or a wig. Then dance.

Of course, there is more to helping out at the Coffee Shop than wearing the apron. A good server makes sure to visit every table. Ask your customers, "What can I get you?" Customers really like free refills, so don't forget to ask.

If you'd prefer being served yourself, just wave down a penguin with a green apron and ask for your drink of choice. Popular drinks include cream soda, hot chocolate, chocolate milk, and iced tea.

Bean Counters!

Being a server in the Coffee Shop is a great way to help out, but you won't earn any coins pouring coffee for customers. To get a paying job, waddle over to the bags of java behind the counter to play *Bean Counters*. You'll be paid in coins to catch the bags of coffee beans as they are tossed from the back of the van and to stack them on the platform.

Catch and Carry: You begin each game with three lives. Move your mouse left and right to get under each bag and catch it. Drop off the bags on the platform by clicking your mouse. Don't carry more than five bags at a time, or you will collapse under the weight!

Earn Coins: Earn points for every bag you catch and drop at the platform. The game has five levels. Every time you reach a new level, you will earn more points for catching and dropping off bags. If you empty all five trucks, you will earn bonus coins.

Avoid Falling Objects: If you get hit by an anvil, fish, or flowerpot, you will also lose a life. If you lose all of your lives, the game ends, but you get to keep the coins you've earned.

GAME TIP

The falling objects are easier to avoid once you know where they fall. The anvil always falls close to the truck, the fish falls close to the platform or in the middle, and the flowerpot falls in the middle. If you get hit, don't worry—catch the shining penguin to earn an extra life!

MANCALA

Mancala is a board game played all over the planet, but you can find it on the top floor of the Coffee Shop in the Book Room. Some penguins are shy about playing *mancala* because it looks a little complicated. It really isn't! The best way to learn is to play a few games. You'll be surprised how quickly you get the hang of it.

Find a Friend: Waddle up to a table and join a penguin waiting to get started, or ask a friend to join you.

Capture Stones: The object of this game is to capture stones and put them in your *mancala*, the big hole on your end of the board. You will take turns with your opponent, trying to capture stones each time. The player who captures the most stones wins.

Develop a Strategy: This takes some practice. Put your mouse over a hole to find out the number of stones in it. Try to plan ahead. If the last stone you drop in a turn lands in your *mancala*, you will receive a free turn.

If All Else Fails, Click: If you're still not sure what to do, don't sweat it. When it's your turn, click on one of the piles of stones on your side. You'll see how the stones move around on the board.

HOW TO PLAY MANCALA

GAME TIP

Try reading the instructions on the wall before you play. That will help, but the best way to get good at *mancala* is to play a few games.

AUNT ARCTIC SAYS

One way to learn how to play a multiplayer game is to watch two other players make their moves. To be a spectator of a game, click on the table while a game is in progress. Be sure to cheer on your friends!

25

PAINT BY LETTERS

If you like to read, this game is for you. You can find it in the Book Room above the Coffee Shop. Go to the bookcase and click on the bookshelf (or click on the red book in the corner of the room). Then click on one of the books with the *Paint By Letters* logo:

Type What You See: When the words appear on a page, start typing them on your computer keyboard. You don't have to worry about capital letters or punctuation. If you miss a letter, you won't be able to move on until you type the letter correctly. As you type, an illustration will appear on the opposite page.

Make It Personal: Sometimes, you'll see two or more words together like this: (one/two/three). Type in the word you'd like to use in the story. This will change the pictures you see.

Earn Coins: You have to finish typing the whole book to earn coins. The longer the book, the more coins you will earn. You won't get penalized for typing mistakes.

GAME TIP

There are bonus coins on almost every illustrated page in the *Paint By Letters* books. Move your mouse around the page to reveal where the coins are hidden. Some are tricky to grab, so keep trying!

Take your puffle for a walk with you when you play the *Paint By Letters* game "My Puffle." The puffle in the story will be the same color as your puffle!

CHECK IT OUT

HOW IT'S DONE

Find the penguin icon on your toolbar and click on it. Move your mouse to the top box, where you'll see a picture of a penguin with music notes around it. Click on this box and get ready to shake and shimmy! Or, for a handy shortcut, click outside of your chat bar and press *D* on your keyboard.

AUNT ARCTIC SAYS

I love secret passageways, don't you? There is one in the Night Club, on the fourth speaker to the right of the door. Click there to find a secret entrance to the Boiler Room.

28

The Night Club

Waddle through the doors of the Night Club and you'll be greeted by the sound of thumping bass pounding out of the speakers. Get up and move to the music on the dance floor, which pulsates with multicolored lights. Or, if you'd rather deejay, step behind the turntables. If the music gets too loud, you can head upstairs— but before you do, make sure to click on the green puffle on the speaker. That little green guy can really groove!

Upstairs in the Dance Lounge is a great place to sit at a table and have a quiet chat with another penguin. It's also where you'll find Club Penguin's old-school arcade games, *Thin Ice* and *Astro-Barrier*. The great thing about them is that you don't have to insert any coins to play—but you can win lots of coins if you've got the skills.

THIN ICE

Puffle fans know that if you feed a black puffle its favorite treat, Puffle-Os, it will turn into a ball of fire. A black puffle on fire is the star of this game. You move the puffle over blocks of ice to complete a maze and earn coins. The more ice blocks you melt, the more coins you'll earn.

Move and Melt: At each level there is a different maze. The object is to move the puffle from the starting point to the end of the maze, a red block. As you move with your keyboard arrows, you will melt the ice blocks you pass over. You can't try to pass over these tiles more than once or you'll sink and start the level all over again.

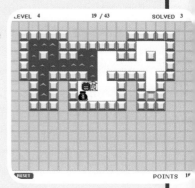

Earn Coins: You can take the easy path each time and finish the maze, but you'll earn more coins if you melt as many tiles as you can.

Special Tiles: There are nineteen mazes in all, and each one is more difficult than the next. In some mazes, the red tile will be blocked by a locked door. You must first grab the key so you can open the door leading to the exit. If you see a light blue block, you can cross over it twice before it melts. Dark blue blocks are moveable, so you can change the way a path runs. And green tiles can transport you to another part of the maze.

GAME TIP

There are coins hidden in the levels of *Thin Ice*. If you complete a level by melting all the ice tiles, a bag of coins will appear in the maze in your next level. Be sure to grab it as you go.

On Level Nineteen there is a false wall in the top right corner of the maze. Move through the false wall until you reach the block with the circle inside it. When you melt this block, an extra bag of coins will appear for every level you have completed. For each bag you grab, you'll earn extra coins.

Astro-Barrier!

There's something really satisfying about shooting objects as they fall from space! This game can be found in the Dance Lounge next to *Thin Ice*.

Move and Shoot: Press the left and right arrow keys to move your ship. Press the space bar to shoot the moving objects overhead.

Make Every Shot Count: If you run out of bullets on a level, you will lose a life. If you keep shooting without aiming, your game will be over pretty quickly.

Plan Your Shots: If a target is hit, it becomes a wall, making it harder to shoot the other targets. One strategy is to hit the targets on top first, then the ones underneath.

Score Points: You earn ten points for each ship you hit, and bonus points each time you clear a level.

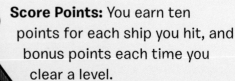

After Level Ten, an instruction box will appear on the screen. Don't hit *enter* to continue playing. Instead, wait twenty-five seconds. A blue ship will appear. Shoot it, and it will lead you to secret levels where you can earn extra points.

DID YOU KNOW?

Once, there was an *Astro-Barrier* T-shirt on sale in the Penguin Style catalog. The shirt was a popular item.

ASTRO-BARRIER

Meet Aunt Arctic

Occupation: Aunt Arctic is the editor in chief of *The Club Penguin Times*, a position she has held since April 2008. Penguins everywhere read her popular weekly column, "Ask Aunt Arctic." Each week she answers questions from penguins. She is also something of a Club Penguin historian and loves keeping up on all the goings-on, which is why she's perfect for giving tips and secrets. And if she doesn't have the answer, she knows how to find out.

Would you like to hear a secret about *me?* The next time you read a newspaper, move your mouse over my eyeglasses. Something *shady* just might happen . . .

AUNT ARCTIC SAYS

PAGE B5
REGULAR FEATURE
ADVICE

ASK AUNT ARCTIC

HELLO YELLOW FELLOW

Dear Aunt Arctic,
Why is there a yellow puffle at The Stage? Who does it belong to?
– Hello Yellow Fellow

Dear Hello Yellow Fellow,
Ever since that little guy showed up during the construction of The Stage, it's been causing quite a stir around the island. While other yellow puffles have been adopted, this one has stuck around The Stage and joined in on many plays and activities there.

Much like the green puffle who makes its home at the Night Club, this yellow puffle appears to be quite happy where it is. If you've seen it appear on stage you know

it can be quite a clown, and audiences everywhere have appreciated its performances.

I suppose as long as there are artistic things happening at The Stage, it'll continue to brighten things up, bringing a smile to its

captivated audience.

ICE ADVICE

Dear Aunt Arctic,
Why is it impossible to melt all the ice on some levels of Thin Ice?
– Ice Advice

Dear Ice Advice,
Thin Ice is one of the more difficult games to master on the island. It takes a great deal of time and skill to figure out each level, and I know only a few penguins that have managed to finish

Continued on next page...

REGULAR FEATURE
PAGE B6

What She Can't Live Without: Her puffles

What Makes Her Smile:
- Penguins who work together and help each other
- Collecting things
- Researching island history
- Decorating her igloo in different themes

Pet Peeves:
- Penguins who tease other penguins
- When her puffles go missing

Favorite Color: Green

Party Penguin: Aunt Arctic never misses a party, and her all-time favorites were the Winter Fiesta of 2007 and the 2007 Fall Fair. She also organized the Easter Scavenger Hunt in 2007.

Easter Scavenger Hunt

When She's Not Working, You Can Find Her:
- In her igloo playing with her beloved puffles
- Sipping hot chocolate in the Coffee Shop

Bet You Didn't Know: Aunt Arctic thinks a certain silly sound that some penguins make is hilarious. (To find out what it is, click outside your chat bar and type "et" on your keyboard.)

There are many ways to express who you are to other penguins. One way is by the things you do, whether you're organizing games of hide-and-seek with your friends, coaching a team at the Ice Rink, or throwing a party in your igloo. Another way you can express yourself is through fashion—and you'll find plenty of it in the Gift Shop.

You'll find two catalogs in the Gift Shop: Big Wigs and Penguin Style. You can combine colors, wigs, backgrounds, clothing, and accessories to show other penguins what you're all about.

Your gear can also let other penguins know how long you've been living on the island. Many catalog items are limited-edition—they come out once, and may not be seen again for a long time. If you see a lucky penguin walking around wearing one of these items, it means they've probably been around a while.

To make sure you don't miss out on any new items, remember that a new Penguin Style catalog is released the first Friday of every month.

Here are some tips for how you can use the catalog items to express yourself:

Match Your Mood: On the first page, all penguins can purchase colors. Changing colors is a simple but effective way to reflect your mood. Feeling angry? Try a fiery red. Mellow? A nice cool blue works well. Cheerful? You can't beat yellow!

Get a Job: In each catalog you'll find at least one item that will let you participate in one of the many jobs on Club Penguin. Buy a lifeguard shirt and head to the Underground Pool or the Cove to keep watch over swimmers. With other items you can be a coffee server, firefighter, construction worker, or more. Don't worry—if you don't see clothes for the job you want now, chances are they will return. Just keep checking.

Wig Out: Sometimes all you need is a new 'do to make a statement. If you have a membership, you can buy a wig from the Big Wigs catalog. Feeling groovy? Then try the Beekeeper (a tall beehive look) or the Disco (a funky 'fro). Feeling beachy? Then maybe the bright yellow Sunstriker is for you.

Personalize Your Player Card: All penguins can buy different backgrounds for their player cards. It's a great way to express your personality, or show others what kind of activities you like to do. If you have a membership, you can also buy a country flag for your player card to show where you're from or where you'd love to visit.

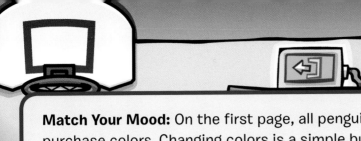

Free Items

Club Penguin's shops aren't the only place you'll find items you can use to express your personality.

- There are always free items given away at official Club Penguin parties.

- Captain Rockhopper often gives away free pirate gear when the *Migrator* docks.

- Complete a scavenger hunt to win free prizes.

- Hidden Pins are available every two weeks and can be used to jazz up your player card. (To find out more about the Hidden Pins, go to page 183.)

TIP

Need coins to buy that sweet bathing suit you've got your eye on? To earn coins quickly, play *Bean Counters* or *Jet Pack Adventure*. You can earn a nice amount of coins playing each game.

AUNT ARCTIC SAYS

There are secret items in every issue of Penguin Style. They are not always easy to find, but I think searching for them is just as much fun as finding them. Move your mouse over the images on each page. The secret items change each month. And you will always find a Viking Helmet hidden somewhere in the catalog.

39

Anything Goes

While some penguins like the sleek look of matching outfits, others have fun by creating the most outrageous looks possible. They combine clothes from Penguin Style and the Sport Shop catalog with free items and costume pieces from The Stage. The result is sometimes weird, sometimes fabulous—and never boring!

Remember, there's no such thing as a "right" or "wrong" outfit, so don't be afraid to come up with as many different combinations as you like. Here are just a few examples of some fashion-forward penguins to give you some ideas.

The Underground

"Let's leave the surface for a while and check out what's underneath the ice: the Underground Pool, the Cave, and the Mine Shaft. These places were first discovered when explorer penguins found underground caves leading to them. Then they went to work, rebuilding them so other penguins could enjoy them. Whether you like to read, swim, or race down a track at breakneck speed, you'll find something to do in the Underground.

"Secret entrances located in the Night Club and the Plaza will bring you to the Boiler Room, which leads to these underground spots. It's a great spot to start the Underground tour."

Old News is Good News: THE BOILER ROOM

You can do more than dance in the Night Club. The fourth speaker on the floor on the right leads to the Boiler Room. Click on it and you will walk down a ladder into the Boiler Room. During the 2008 April Fool's Day Party the Boiler Room became a boiling room—literally! A big vat of boiling water steamed things up in this underground room.

The steamy room is filled with old wooden crates and green file cabinets. Those cabinets contain a real treasure: past issues of *The Club Penguin Times*. You'll find other penguins hanging out here and reading back issues of the paper. Join them and become a Club Penguin expert by catching up on tips and secrets, past parties, and any other news you might have missed.

April Fool's Day

Indoor Swimming:
THE UNDERGROUND POOL

Walk through the green door in the Boiler Room and you'll be in the Cave—a cool underwater hangout. You'll see penguins getting their flippers wet in the pool. Some might be dressed in bathing suits, scuba gear, mermaid costumes, or life jackets and snorkels. Others might be hanging out by the side of the pool, watching the strange creatures that swim past the windows. You can even climb into the lifeguard chair and watch over your fellow penguins as they splash around.

The pool is a great place to get some exercise. Invite some friends to do laps with you, or even race one another. Or the next time you want to throw a party, why not throw a pool party? Head into town or some other crowded place and invite other penguins to join you at the pool.

AUNT ARCTIC SAYS

After a long day of writing, I love to relax with a refreshing dip in the pool. You, too, can swim in the pool, thanks to a few clothing items. Wear the water wings, inflatable duck, or green inflatable duck, and dance, and you will swim. These items were given out for free at parties.

DID YOU KNOW?

There's a shortcut to the Cave in the Plaza. Just click on the manhole cover in front of the Pet Shop. You'll be doing the backstroke in no time.

One of the craziest accidents in Club Penguin history happened at the pool in July 2007. It was just another day at the pool until a crab tapped on one of the glass windows at the pool and accidentally broke it. Water poured in, causing the entire Underground to flood! (Crabs always seem to be causing trouble. If you've ever played *Ice Fishing*, you'll know why.)

Luckily, penguins always look on the bright side and figured out how to turn a disaster into a good time. They threw a huge water party! Penguins ran hoses from the Underground to the surface of the island to drain the flood, and lots of fun followed. There were water balloons, water polo, and big fishbowls for igloos. Giant inflatable animals squirted out water in different spots around the island—like a blue whale at the Iceberg. The party was such a blast that penguins still talk about it today.

In the Dark:
THE CAVE AND THE MINE SHACK

Don't be afraid to waddle through the dark tunnel on the right-hand side of the pool. It will lead you to the Cave. A shadowy and quiet place, the Cave is lit by a single lantern. Don't be spooked! You can have a lot of fun here hanging with your pals or playing *Cart Surfer* in the Mine Shaft.

Many penguins remember when the Mine opened for the first time in May 2006. Penguins love a reason to celebrate, so there was a huge underground party! Everyone gathered together to explore this new place. Mining helmets became available for the first time then. Penguins discovered that when they danced while wearing their helmets, they could drill into the hard rock. Penguins quickly formed drilling parties and started to break ground.

Today, mining and construction helmets are worn by penguins and wherever something new is being built, you can find groups of penguins with their helmets on, drilling away. In fact, many penguins like to hang out in the Mine and practice their drilling skills so they'll be ready for the next big construction project!

The next time a new construction project is going on, gather up your friends, put on your helmets, and help out. If you like being a leader, take on the role of crew foreman. You can tell your crew where to drill, when to work, and when to take breaks.

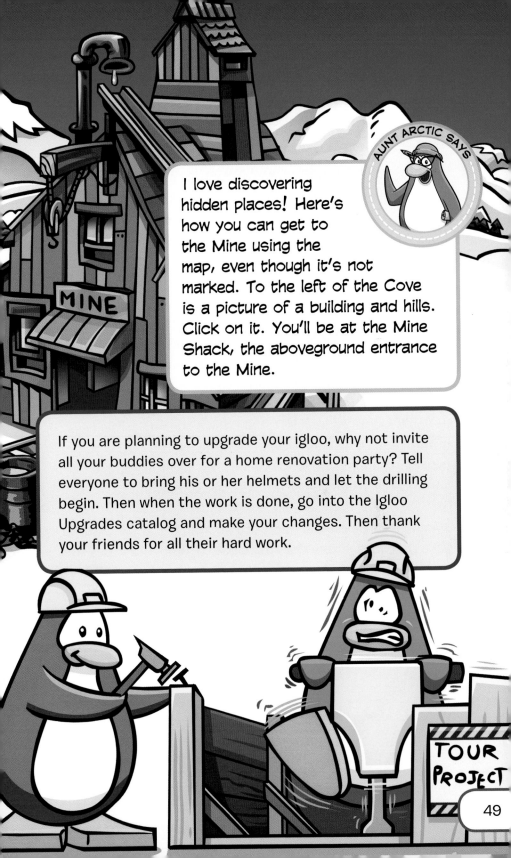

I love discovering hidden places! Here's how you can get to the Mine using the map, even though it's not marked. To the left of the Cove is a picture of a building and hills. Click on it. You'll be at the Mine Shack, the aboveground entrance to the Mine.

If you are planning to upgrade your igloo, why not invite all your buddies over for a home renovation party? Tell everyone to bring his or her helmets and let the drilling begin. Then when the work is done, go into the Igloo Upgrades catalog and make your changes. Then thank your friends for all their hard work.

MINE

TOUR PROJECT

49

CART SURFER!!

Hop aboard a mine cart for a wild ride! In this fast-paced game you travel at high speeds through the Mine. To play, enter the Mine and walk to the mining carts.

How to Play:

Away You Go!: Not much time to think with this game—as soon as it starts your cart is off for a wild ride! Hold on tight and try to make it through without tipping over.

Tricky Turns: When you see a turn coming up, lean into it or you'll crash! To lean left, hold down the left arrow key, and to lean right, hold down the right. Watch out: If you lean for too long you will wipe out. Be careful! You get three carts. Once you're out, the game is over.

Mining for Tricks: The secret to scoring big at *Cart Surfer* is to do tricks. Press the space bar to jump and press the up and down arrows to try different moves. But don't try to do a stunt while turning or you will crash! The more tricks you do, the more coins you'll earn.

DID YOU KNOW?

If you finish *Cart Surfer,* you will end the game aboveground, at the Mine Shack. If you wipe out too many times, you'll stay belowground!

Cart Surfer is one exciting ride. I've got to hold on to my hat when I play it! I love to try new tricks, but sometimes learning them can be a bit tricky. The best way to figure out how to do different tricks is to try different combinations with your arrow keys and space bar. Here are two tricks to get you started:

- 360° Turn: Hit the space bar and then the left or right arrow key.

- Backflip: Press the down arrow and then space bar.

The Plaza

"There's always something new and exciting going on in the Plaza. Penguins who love pizza, pets, and play flock to the Plaza every day.

"The first stop there is the Pet Shop, where you can adopt a puffle. Next door you'll find The Stage, where you can star in a play—or just sit back and watch the show. And if all that entertainment makes you hungry, follow the smell of cheese to the Pizza Parlor. Besides being a great place to grab a bite to eat, it's also one of the hottest spots on Club Penguin."

Back in November 2005, an unusual creature was discovered hiding out in the Snow Forts. It was a puffle—a round, furry animal that lived in the wilds of Club Penguin. More puffles appeared, and penguins began rounding up the friendly little guys. A few months later you could adopt your very own puffle in the Pet Shop!

If your igloo is a little lonely, waddle over to the Pet Shop to find a companion you can play with and take care of. At the Pet Shop you can adopt a puffle, buy supplies for your pet, and even earn some coins by getting a job there!

Puffles make loyal, friendly pets. Adopt one, treat it right, and you'll have a friend for life. But if you don't take care of your puffle, it might run away!

Puffles need to be fed, bathed, taken for walks, and played with. Puffles come in different colors, and each color has its own personality, favorite toys, and special features. If you are a penguin without a membership, you can adopt up to two puffles: two blue, two red, or one of each. Players with memberships can adopt as many as fourteen, in every color available.

But before you start adopting lots of puffles, make sure you have enough coins to take care of them properly. Not only does it cost 800 coins to adopt each puffle, but you will need additional coins every time you want to feed and bathe your puffle.

Puffle Personalities

Puffles make the perfect pets. I adore mine! Here's a tip for puffle owners. If you have a membership when you adopt your puffles but your membership ends, you get to keep all of your pets. Your other items will be taken away and put into storage, and you can access them if you get a membership again. But your puffles are always yours, no matter what!

BLUE PUFFLE

Attitude: Mild-tempered, content, loyal
Favorite toy: Ball
Special features: Loyal, easy to take care of

RED PUFFLE

Attitude: Adventurous, enthusiastic
Favorite toys: Bowling pins, cannon
Special feature: Originally from Rockhopper Island

PINK PUFFLE

Attitude: Active, cheery
Favorite toys: Jump rope, trampoline
Special feature: Loves to exercise

BLACK PUFFLE

Attitude: Strong, silent type
Favorite toy: Skateboard
Special feature: Sometimes very energetic

GREEN PUFFLE

Attitude: Energetic, playful
Favorite toys: Unicycle, propeller cap
Special feature: Likes to clown around

PURPLE PUFFLE

Attitude: A bit of a diva, picky eater
Favorite toys: Bubble wand, disco ball
Special feature: Loves to dance

YELLOW PUFFLE

Attitude: Artistic, spontaneous
Favorite toys: Paintbrush, easel
Special features: Very creative, dreamer

Puffle Personality Test

How can you tell which puffle is right for you? Take the Club Penguin Puffle Personality Test and find out now!

Which one of these is your favorite Club Penguin hangout?
   a. The Night Club
   b. The Ice Rink
   c. The Stage
   d. The Coffee Shop
   e. The Dojo
   f. The Beach or the Cove
   g. Your igloo

What is your favorite after-school activity?
   a. Listening to music
   b. Playing any kind of sport
   c. Clowning around with my friends
   d. Drawing or painting
   e. Skateboarding
   f. Surfing, boating, or swimming
   g. Watching television

Out of these jobs, which do you think you'd like the best?
   a. Dancer
   b. Athlete
   c. Comedian
   d. Artist
   e. Professional skateboarder
   f. Pirate
   g. They all sound like fun!

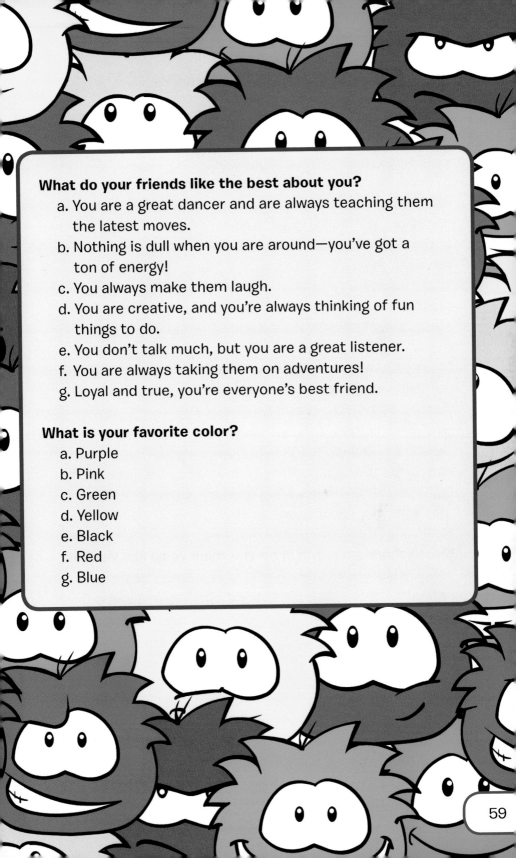

What do your friends like the best about you?
a. You are a great dancer and are always teaching them the latest moves.
b. Nothing is dull when you are around—you've got a ton of energy!
c. You always make them laugh.
d. You are creative, and you're always thinking of fun things to do.
e. You don't talk much, but you are a great listener.
f. You are always taking them on adventures!
g. Loyal and true, you're everyone's best friend.

What is your favorite color?
a. Purple
b. Pink
c. Green
d. Yellow
e. Black
f. Red
g. Blue

Your Puffle Personality

Mostly As: A purple puffle is perfect for you! These puffles are happiest when they are dancing, so make sure to take your purple puffle to the Night Club.

Mostly Bs: A pink puffle is perfect for you! This active and happy puffle is a great athlete. Take your pink puffle anywhere on the island where there is lots of room to run around!

Mostly Cs: A green puffle is perfect for you! This playful puffle loves to clown around and will keep you laughing.

Mostly Ds: A yellow puffle is perfect for you! This creative puffle likes to paint. You'll love seeing the masterpieces your yellow puffle creates for you.

Mostly Es: A black puffle is perfect for you! Quiet and independent, black puffles like to keep to themselves. But if you like skateboarding as much as black puffles do, they'll be your friends for life.

Mostly Fs: A red puffle is perfect for you! An adventurous penguin like you needs a puffle who is up for anything. A red puffle can explore right along with you and can even go surfing with you.

Mostly Gs: A blue puffle is perfect for you! Laid-back and loyal, this easy-to-take-care-of puffle is a lot like you. Walk your blue puffle around Club Penguin or just hang out in your igloo. Either way, it will be happy!

If you tied between two letters, don't worry. You'll just have to adopt more than one puffle to make sure you get the perfect pet!

Adopting a Puffle

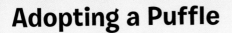

You'll need 800 coins to adopt a puffle. When you are ready, go into the Pet Shop and click on the pen with all the puffles in it. Or you can click on the red book in the lower right-hand corner. Both will open up the Adopt a Puffle catalog for you. Look through it and decide which puffle you want. Then click on *Adopt*. You'll be asked to name your puffle right away. Choose carefully—once you name your puffle, you can't change the name. When you do make your choice, your new puffle pal will be waiting for you inside your igloo!

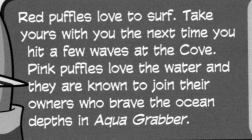

CHECK IT OUT

Red puffles love to surf. Take yours with you the next time you hit a few waves at the Cove. Pink puffles love the water and they are known to join their owners who brave the ocean depths in *Aqua Grabber*.

Caring for Your Puffle

Click on your puffle to view its puffle player card. This will let you know if your pet is hungry, healthy, happy, or needs rest. The picture of your puffle will let you know what kind of mood it is in: If it is smiling, keep up the good work! If your puffle is wearing a frown, try to see what is wrong with it. The three bars on the puffle player card can help you figure out how to make your puffle happier and healthier. The bars represent energy, health, and rest. The lower the bars, the more attention your puffle needs in that area. For instance, if your puffle needs some sleep, the bar for rest will be lower. Food, baths, and playing with your puffle can keep its energy and health bars full. Here's all you need to know to keep your puffle happy and healthy:

Play: Click on the ⊗ on your puffle's player card to play with your pet. Puffles like to play in different ways. Some like to draw while others like to blow bubbles. It all depends on what color they are. Playing with your puffle keeps it happy and in good shape. But if your puffle is too tired or too hungry, it won't have the energy to play with you!

Catch Some Zzzs: Puffles are very active creatures who love to play but also need a lot of rest. Make sure your puffle gets enough sleep. Click on the Ⓩ on the puffle player card. Your pet will take a quick nap and its rest bar will be full. Then it will be ready to explore Club Penguin with you! But be careful not to give your puffle too many naps. Too much sleep can make its health bar go down.

Chow Down: To keep your puffle's energy bar full, make sure it gets enough food. Click on the  on the puffle player card to feed your pet. A new window will open and you'll be able to give your pet bubble gum, a cookie, or a bowl of nutritious Puffle-Os. You will need coins to pay for these treats.

Bubble gum and cookies are given to puffles as special treats. Puffles will do a special trick for you when you give them some, but only if they are happy. If your pet is sad, it will stick out its tongue at you instead! Don't feed too many of these snacks to your puffles. If they are too full, they won't eat them.

A box of tasty Puffle-Os is the perfect way to fill up your puffle's energy bar. Even though your puffle might look super cute when it is gobbling up its food, do not overfeed it. If you try to feed it when its energy bar is full, its health bar will go down!

Bath Time: Keep your puffle clean and healthy by giving it a bath. Click on the food tab. Your puffle will be clean in no time!

Go for a Walk: Your puffle can explore Club Penguin with you. Simply click on 🌀 on the puffle player card to walk your puffle. Your puffle can dance with you at the Night Club, dodge snowballs with you at the Snow Forts, and go shopping with you.

If your puffle is tired and hungry it may refuse to walk with you. Only one puffle can go for a walk at a time. Make sure you don't have any other hand items on, such as a bracelet or a fishing pole, or you won't be able to walk your puffle. When the walk is over, open your player card and click on your puffle. The puffle will go back to your igloo. You might want to check and make sure that your puffle isn't tired or hungry from its walk. It might need a snack or a nap after all the excitement of traveling around Club Penguin.

Runaway Puffle!: Owning a puffle is a lot of fun—but also a lot of hard work! When you are not in your igloo, your puffle will still get hungry, tired, and want attention. To have the happiest puffles around, make sure to check on them regularly.

When you log off of Club Penguin, you don't have to worry about your puffle. It will go into pause mode and stay exactly how you left it until you return. Your puffle will not get tired or hungry or run away.

But when you are logged in, don't ignore your puffle. If you stop taking care of your puffle it will get bored and go back to the wilderness. But don't worry. If this happens, your puffle will be nice and safe in the wild. After all, that's where it came from!

Gifts for Your Puffle: Players with memberships can buy some really cool puffle gear at the Pet Shop. Click on the orange book in the bottom-right corner to view the Love Your Pet: Pet Furniture catalog. You can purchase puffle houses, beds, dishes, and toys. You can even buy your puffle an igloo of its very own. Don't worry. If you don't have the coins to totally spoil your puffle, you can still keep it happy by taking good care of it.

When you do purchase an item for your puffle, it will automatically be put in storage in your igloo. (To learn more about decorating your igloo, go to page 146.)

To learn more about decorating your igloo, go to page 146.

DID YOU KNOW?

If puffles seem like too much work, you can buy easier-to-care-for pets at the Pet Shop such as goldfish, birds, and turtles if you have a membership. You add them to your igloo like any piece of furniture. While caring for one of these pets is a breeze, the downside is they are not nearly as fun and entertaining as a puffle!

PUFFLE ROUND-UP

If you love puffles, why not get a job at the Pet Shop? Go to the door marked "Employees" and help herd the puffles back into their pen. Coins are awarded based on how many puffles you can catch in the shortest amount of time.

How to Play:

Start Herding: Use your mouse to guide puffles into the fenced area. If you want the puffle to move right, place your mouse to the left of the puffle. If you want the puffle to go left, put your mouse on the right. Trying to get a puffle to move down? Put your mouse on top of it and move it around! To get a puffle to move up, put your mouse below it.

Be Careful!: Puffles can be pretty tricky. Some will run away before you can get them into their pen. Try not to steer the puffle off the screen.

The More You Herd, the More You Earn: A round ends when all the puffles have been herded or have run away. You can end the game after any round. Keep playing to get lots of puffle herding practice, and earn lots of coins, too!

If you are the type of penguin who wants to see your name in lights, head over to The Stage! You and your penguin buddies can star in a play. Not interested in being a leading penguin? Sit back and watch, or volunteer to work the lights, be the director, sell tickets, or be an usher. It takes a lot of penguins to put on a great show!

You can star in everything from a science-fiction space adventure to a play about a high school pep rally. If you want to know what's playing, just look at the marquee outside the theater. Plays change every month.

Before and After

At one time, the Plaza had a great Pet Shop and a delicious Pizza Parlor, but it was missing some entertainment. Construction began and curious penguins wondered what the new addition to the Plaza would be. In November 2007, The Stage was unveiled. Penguins have been taking bows there ever since!

Before

After

AUNT ARCTIC SAYS

Watching a good play is such a pleasant way to pass the time. I applaud all the penguins who work hard to put on these productions. My advice for would-be actors is to use your imagination! Some of the best plays I have ever seen were when penguins wrote their own scripts. Use the provided script for inspiration—then get creative and come up with your own ideas. I'm sure it will be a hit!

How to Put on a Play

Here's what you need to know to put on a spectacular show:

Get Your Buddies Together: If you're hanging out with your buddies, send a postcard inviting your buddies to The Stage. Once you are there, decide which roles everyone will take.

Be an Actor: Inside the theater you'll see two icons on the bottom right of the page: a Costume catalog and a script. In the script you will see the names of the characters in the play, and their lines. Choose which role you want to play. If you have a membership, you can use the Costume catalog to outfit yourself for the role. Head for The Stage and open the script. Click on your lines and you will read them onstage.

Be a Director: Every great production needs a director with a vision. If you like taking charge, go to the Costume catalog. Players with a membership can buy a director's cap. Put it on and help guide the actors. You can let them know when to begin and where to stand. (You'll even find lines in the script to give you ideas of what you can say.)

Be a Stagehand: Put the *special* into the special effects of your play by being a stagehand. Waddle over to the Switchbox 3000. Click the buttons and pull the levers to control the sets, turn on spotlights, and create special effects!

Be an Usher: Make sure everyone is seated for the big show. You can escort penguins to their seats and show them how to get into the balcony.

Be in the Orchestra: Buy an instrument in the Penguin Style catalog if you don't already have one and get together with other musicians. Then head to the black area in front of The Stage. It's called the Pit. You can turn any play into a musical by adding an orchestra!

Be a Ticket Taker: Once you've decided who is doing what, you need an audience to watch your fabulous show. If you'd like to be a ticket taker, hang out behind the ticket window in the front of the theater. When a penguin approaches, ask, "Would you like a ticket?" Or just greet them with a smile. You'll soon have curious penguins lining up to check out your play!

Relax and Enjoy the Show: Sit back and be entertained! Let other penguins know if you like the show by using your emoticons.

More Things to Do at The Stage

There's no rule that says you have to put on a play at The Stage. It's a great space with lights, cool sets, and plenty of seats for spectators. Penguins have come up with great ideas for using The Stage in other ways. What ideas can you come up with? Here are just a few:

- Have a snowball fight there.

- Hold a costume contest. Mix and match costumes from the Costume catalog. Penguin judges use emotes to show if they like or dislike your costume.

- Use the space for your band practice.

- Hold a poetry reading. Get your poetry-writing buddies together or make an announcement in the Town Center. Penguins take The Stage one at a time to recite original poems.

DID YOU KNOW?

When The Stage was first built, a yellow puffle was hiding there. This was before you could adopt a yellow puffle. If you moved your mouse over the two puffles on the wooden plaque on the top of The Stage, a yellow one would appear in the balcony. Penguins everywhere came to The Stage to check it out. Today, you can find the yellow puffle in every play—it always takes on a part.

Encore, Encore!

These plays were hits! Maybe we'll see them again one day.

Space Adventure: A captain and crew blast off to Planet X in search of alien life. They find it!

Squidzoid vs. Shadow Guy and Gamma Girl: A giant squid attacks, and it's Shadow Guy and Gamma Girl to the rescue!

Team Blue's Rally Debut: Who will win the mascot tryouts? The Stage was transformed into a high school gymnasium to find out in this theatrical production.

The Twelfth Fish: To fish or not to fish, that is the question. Leave it to a bunch of penguins to turn fishing into a Shakespearean play!

Quest for the Golden Puffle: Can an explorer survive breaking bridges, snowball attacks, and crocodiles to discover the mysterious golden puffle statue?

The Penguins That Time Forgot: Chester gets his flippers on a time machine. He takes the boxlike creation back to his igloo and steps into it. The rest is, as they say, prehistory.

Penguins who love pizza and games flock to one of the most popular places around: the Pizza Parlor!

Step inside the doors and breathe deeply—the air is filled with the smell of yummy pizzas baking in the brick oven. Tables and chairs are everywhere, inviting penguins to sit down and enjoy a pizza with their friends. How you spend your time in the Pizza Parlor is up to you. You can help out, hang out, or earn coins by playing *Pizzatron 3000*.

There's a lot of work to do in the Pizza Parlor. If you want to help out, just jump in as a waiter, cashier, pizza chef, or even a bouncer. That's right—a bouncer! Don't get too rowdy or rude in the Pizza Parlor or another penguin might ask you to leave.

A workforce this big needs a manager. You'll often discover that a penguin will take over the role of boss, hiring workers and giving out assignments. Most of the time the manager will stand behind the cash register, giving out orders to all the employees. If you think you've got what it takes to be management material, give it a shot. But remember to be fair and give everyone an equal turn!

You'll see penguins tossing pizza dough into the air here—these are the pizza chefs. Players with a membership can buy a chef's hat from the clothing catalog. Put it on and then waddle over to the Pizza Parlor and click on the *dance* action on your toolbar. You will start tossing pizza dough. If this doesn't work, make sure you're not wearing any other clothes items. Even something small like a bracelet will stop you from tossing dough. (To learn more about special *dance* actions, go to page 182.)

Of course, instead of working, you can just chill out in this comfy café. Take a seat and chat with a friend. If you get hungry, remember to use your pizza emoticon. A waiter or chef should stop by and take your order!

TIP

Looking for the chef's hat? To find it, keep checking the clothing catalog. A new job is featured each month.

PIZZATRON 3000

How does a spicy seaweed pizza sound? Or how about a flamethrower fish pizza? Hungry penguins from all over flock to the Pizza Parlor to eat these special pies. You can earn lots of coins if your pizza-making skills are fast enough to feed them! Go through the doorway with the beaded curtains and straight into the kitchen to get started.

How to Play:

Order Up: A pizza crust will slide by you on the conveyor belt. It's up to you to add the toppings to get the order right. Look at the order screen in the top right-hand corner to see what kind of pizza you have to make.

The Perfect Pizza: Drag and drop items onto the pizza crust. Your customers will request anything from pizza sauce, hot sauce, cheese, seaweed, shrimp, fish, squid, or a combination of these toppings.

Oops!: If you made a mistake on a pizza, it won't sell, but you'll get the chance to make it again. If you make five mistakes, penguins will stop buying your pizza and it's game over!

Earn Extra Coins: After you make five perfect pizzas in a row, you start to earn tips from happy customers. Your first tip is ten coins. If you keep making pizzas without making mistakes, your tips will increase.

Fast Fingers: As the game progresses, the pizzas get more complicated—and the conveyor belt speeds up! Pay attention and move fast to get all your orders done right.

GAME TIP

Before you start making pizzas, look for the red lever on the conveyor belt. Click on it and then press start. You'll be making pizzas topped with chocolate sauce, icing, sprinkles, and chocolate chips!

The Forest and the Cove

"Penguins love to head out into the great outdoors and throw a party! Come with me and I'll show you two perfect party spots: the Forest and the Cove.

"These places were first discovered by penguins in May 2007. Two explorers lost their map, and penguins went on a scavenger hunt to find it. When the map was recovered, penguins followed the path it showed and it led them right here. You'll find that there's plenty of room for all your friends in the Forest. The Forest leads to the Cove, the perfect spot for a beach bash extravaganza."

Nature lovers alert! You can clear your thoughts, admire the pine trees, and breathe the fresh, clean air in the Forest. Usually a peaceful and secluded spot, the Forest is a nice place to stroll through on your way to the Cove. This outdoor spot is filled with snow-covered trees. You can get to the Forest by following the path to the right of the Plaza or from the map. If you'd like a quiet place to chat with a friend, you can do it at the Forest.

Sometimes the Forest is anything but quiet. It's a nice roomy spot—which makes it the perfect place to throw a party. You can invite all your buddies—or you can wait for an official Club Penguin party. Interesting things can happen in the Forest during one of these monthly shindigs. At the Halloween Party of October 2007, the Forest was transformed into a spooky wilderness. Penguins could hide inside trees and jump out and scare their friends! At the Fiesta Party in January 2008, you could have a yummy treat at the Churro and Ice Cream Hut.

Halloween Party

Fiesta Party

TIP

Want to take your puffle surfing?
You can if you own a red puffle! Simply
take your red puffle for a walk and head
to *Catchin' Waves*. It will hang ten on its
very own surfboard right next to you!

At this hot beach spot you'll find penguins gathered around a roaring fire, sitting on logs, and swapping stories. You'll often see a penguin perched in the lifeguard chair, keeping a watchful eye over the swimmers. The rustic surf shack has surfboards stacked up against it, just waiting for a penguin to hang ten. Whether you are ready for some action or just want to chill out, the Cove has it all.

Lifeguards Wanted: Swimmers dressed in the latest bathing suit styles come to splash around in the Cove. If you'd like to protect other penguins, hop into the lifeguard chair. You can look through the binoculars and keep watch for any dangers that could be lurking out at sea. On a normal day you'll see penguins playing *Hydro-Hopper* and fish leaping out of the water. Be ready to put down those binoculars and race to the rescue of any swimmers who might be in distress.

Warm Up!: Gather up your friends and take a seat at the campfire. This is the perfect spot to have a ghost-story-telling contest. Find out which of your friends can tell the spookiest story around the fire. You may see some penguins roasting marshmallows on sticks. The sticks were first given away at the Camp Penguin Party held in August 2007.

Surf's Up: After the Cove was discovered, one penguin who loved to surf saw the perfect opportunity to ride the waves off the shore of the newly discovered beach. But he needed a place to store his boards and so he went to work, building the Surf Hut. Surfers have been flocking there ever since. You'll often see them hanging out here, dressed in all kinds of beach fashions, usually with a surfboard tucked under their flipper. Head over to the Gift Shop, look for some cool beachwear, and go hang ten with your new surfer buddies.

Cowabunga! Head over to the Surf Hut (the hut that says "Surf" on it) to shoot the tube, get huge air, and perform totally tubular tricks. It takes practice to become a good surfer so don't give up. Expect to wipe out a few times before you get the hang of it.

How to Play:

Getting Started: Choose from Surf Lesson, Freestyle, Competition, and Survival. If it's your first time, take the Surf Lesson and you'll be surfing like a pro in no time. Experienced surfers suggest that you practice in Freestyle mode before you move on to Competition and Survival.

Hanging Ten: Use your mouse to steer up and down, lean forward and back, and to keep your balance.

Tubular Tricks: Use your keyboard to perform tricks. You can press either the *W, A, S, D* keys or the arrow keys while you are surfing. Try pressing different combinations of keys to perform advanced tricks.

"Shoot the tube" by surfing very close to the curl of the wave. Don't get too close to the wave or you'll end up wiping out!

Coins at the Cove: The more tricks you do, the more coins you will earn, so visit the Cove often and keep on *Catchin' Waves*!

Basic Moves:

Wave	(UP Key, or *W* Key)
Sit	(DOWN Key, or *S* Key)
Handstand	(LEFT Key, or *A* Key)
Dance	(RIGHT Key, or *D* Key)

**To do advanced moves,
combine one basic move with another.**

Advanced Moves:

The Lazy Wave	(UP + DOWN) OR (*W* + *S*) (Wave + Sit)
Coastal Kick	(LEFT + RIGHT) OR (*A* + *D*) (Handstand + Dance)
The Backstand	(DOWN + LEFT) OR (*S* + *A*) (Sit + Handstand)
Surf Fever	(RIGHT +UP) OR (*D* + *W*) (Dance + Wave)
Ice Breaker	(LEFT + UP) OR (*A* + *W*) (Handstand + Wave)
Blender	(DOWN + RIGHT) OR (*S* + *D*) (Sit + Dance)

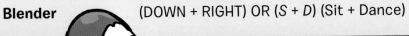

Bring Your Own Board

Head over to the Sport Shop located in the Ski Village and look through the Snow and Sports catalog to pick out a brand-new surfboard. To use it when playing *Catchin' Waves*, enter the game while holding it. Using your own board can increase your speed so you can earn more points while doing tricks.

AUNT ARCTIC SAYS

I like to surf in style, and my silver surfboard fits the bill. If you've never come across this special board before, I'll let you in on a shopping secret. Go to the Sport Shop and click on the Snow and Sports catalog. When you come to the page with the surfboards, click on the picture of the penguin holding one. The surfboard will change color. Then click on the starfish on the lower left-hand corner, and then the seashell on the lower right. The penguin will now be holding the silver surfboard and you'll get the chance to buy it for 800 coins. Make sure you are holding it the next time you play *Catchin' Waves* and you'll be surfing on your new board!

Forts, Rink, and Dock

"Penguins love to be outside, especially when it's cold and snowy out. Let's check out some of the best spots for outdoor activities: the Dock, the Ice Rink, and the Snow Forts. Whether you're into sports or you just like to play in the snow, you're sure to find some fun in these outdoor areas."

Hangin' By the Water: THE DOCK

Take the path to the right of the Lighthouse. It leads to the Dock, a great place to go fishing, play *Hydro-Hopper*, or just hang out and catch some rays.

For past parties the Dock has been transformed into an ice-skating rink, a snow castle, and even a pumpkin patch.

HYDRO-HOPPER

Grab a tube and hold on tight as a speedboat tows you in *Hydro-Hopper*! This game used to be known as *Ballistic Biscuit* until September 2007. Waddle over to the speedboat next to the Dock to get started. The object of the game is to avoid obstacles and earn more coins by jumping over anything in your way.

Avoid Sharks: . . . and icebergs, seagulls, floating logs, or anything else in the water. If you don't, you will crash and fall out of your tube. Use your mouse to move and click to jump. Move to the left and right to stay away from drifting objects or jump over them.

Buoy Bother: You can't jump over buoys—they are too tall. Avoid them instead.

Look for Life Preservers: Pick one up to earn an extra life.

Earn Extra Coins: Jumping over an object rather than just steering clear will earn you more coins. Try jumping over two objects at once to earn even more!

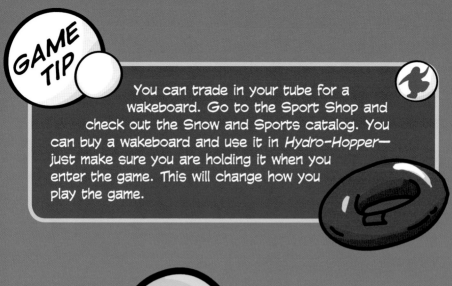

GAME TIP

You can trade in your tube for a wakeboard. Go to the Sport Shop and check out the Snow and Sports catalog. You can buy a wakeboard and use it in *Hydro-Hopper*—just make sure you are holding it when you enter the game. This will change how you play the game.

Snowball Fight: THE SNOW FORTS

Penguins love throwing snowballs, and they do it just about anywhere: in the Pizza Parlor, at The Stage, in the Mine, and even in their own igloos. But the best place for a serious snowball fight is definitely the Snow Forts.

You'll find two forts there: one with a pink flag, and one with a blue flag. Pick a fort and start throwing snowballs. Once a snowball fight begins, other penguins will usually show up to join in the fun.

To throw a snowball, click on the ⊚ on your toolbar. A target will appear on the screen. Move the target to the place where you want your snowball to land, and click. You will throw a snowball!

At the Snow Forts, you'll find the snowball-powered clock. All the other clocks on Club Penguin are set to the same time as the Clock Tower. Gary the Gadget Guy built the clock in February 2007. He designed it so when penguins aimed a snowball at the target attached to it, the inner gears would wind up.

The clock is set to PST—Penguin Standard Time. PST might be different than the time on your computer, but every penguin on the island will see the same PST on the clock. That makes it easier to schedule meet-ups with your buddies.

CLUB PENGUIN TIME ZONE

3:42 PM

WEDNESDAY

CHECK IT OUT

You will see penguins throwing snowballs in other places, even indoors. Around here, it's another friendly way of saying hello. If you're not interested in a snowball fight, simply walk away, or say, "No, thanks."

AUNT ARCTIC SAYS

Use a keyboard shortcut to throw snowballs more quickly. Put your cursor over the spot you'd like to hit and press the *T* key on your keyboard. (Make sure your cursor is not inside the chat bar, or this will not work.) A target will appear. Click to throw a snowball, and then keep pressing *T* to throw a bunch of snowballs, one after the other.

Feeling competitive? Head down to the Ice Rink, where there's always some kind of game going on. Any penguin can play the games here. If you'd rather sit on the sidelines, there's always room in the stands for a new spectator. Or, if you have a membership, buy a cheerleader outfit in the Snow and Sports catalog and cheer on the players!

The games at the Ice Rink are just for fun—you can't earn coins by playing them. Games can change with the seasons or during special events and parties, but the basic way to play them is the same: Use your mouse to move around the playing field. Skate into the ball or puck to send it flying across the ice. Take turns with other penguins playing different positions.

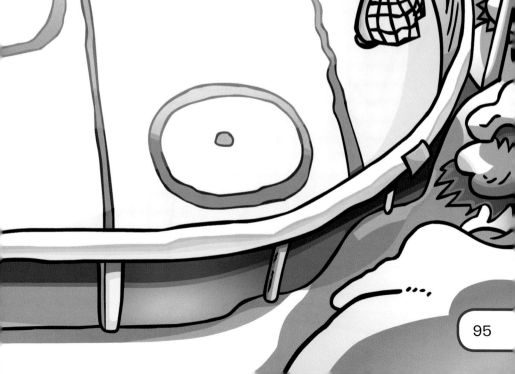

Spotlight: Ice Hockey

Here are a few tips, in case you want to start a game:

1. If you have a membership, head to the Sport Shop and purchase a hockey stick, helmet, and uniform. You don't have to wear these objects to play, but suiting up before a game can help psych you up!

2. Send a postcard to your buddies and ask them to meet you in the Ice Rink. If none of your buddies are online, go to the Ice Rink and join the other players there.

3. Divide up into teams. This can be as easy as simply moving to one side of the rink or the other. You and your teammates can also change your colors so you all match. Popular team colors are blue and red. Some teams get serious and assign positions to each player. Your game can be more casual than that, but make sure one penguin on each team is there to protect the goal.

4. If the puck is not already in the center of the rink, knock it into one of the nets. It will automatically appear in the center. Have two penguins face off, and it's game on!
Basically, all you have to do is go after the puck and get it into the opposite goal. To slide across the ice, click and hold down your mouse as you move it across the rink. If you bump into the puck, it will move. If you get the puck into the goal, it will appear in the center of the rink again.

The Beach and the Migrator

"The Beach and the Dock are two places you can go if you're craving a little fun in the sun. You can lounge with friends in beach chairs, explore the Lighthouse, fly at *Jet Pack Adventure*, and ride the waves in *Hydro-Hopper*.

Every once in a while you'll see Rockhopper's ship, the *Migrator*, docked here. The captain himself comes ashore when he's docked to make new friends. Keep an eye out—you just might spot him."

Room with a View:
THE LIGHTHOUSE AND THE BEACON

Waddle over to the Beach and you can't miss the Lighthouse. Inside this tall building is the perfect spot to hold a concert with your band. Use instruments you've bought in the Penguin Style catalog, or hop behind the piano or the microphone and drums onstage. Before you play, make sure to go into Town Center and invite everyone to the show.

When you're done jamming, head for the staircase. The wall is covered with pictures and maps. See anyone's portrait you know?

When you reach the top you'll discover the Beacon at the top of the Lighthouse. Its light guides ships, like the *Migrator*, safely to Club Penguin shores. Hop on the platform to see if the *Migrator*—or anything else—is headed toward the island.

The Beacon is in shipshape now, but back in 2006 it needed a lot of repairs. Penguins donated their coins to help restore it, and soon the Lighthouse was better than ever. The restoration came just in time—Rockhopper saw the light welcoming him in after a long voyage lost at sea.

The Beacon

You might not be able to sail the seas with Rockhopper, but you can soar through the skies if you play *Jet Pack Adventure*. In this game, you blast off from the top of the Beacon.

Make sure to check out the Lighthouse and the Beacon during parties and holidays. One Halloween, the bulb of the Beacon was turned into a giant jack-o'-lantern, and for Christmas 2006, it was a huge Christmas light. The entire Lighthouse has been turned into a palm tree for past summer parties and then transformed again in December 2007 into a giant Christmas tree.

The Beacon at Halloween

JET PACK ADVENTURE

Thanks to Gary the Gadget Guy, penguins are able to take to the skies in the high-flying game *Jet Pack Adventure*. Soar through the skies collecting coins on the way. Whatever coins you get, you keep!

The Good and the Bad Stuff: Use your arrow keys to control your jet pack. Try to fly into coins, fuel, and extra jet packs. Avoid anvils, coffee bags, trees, and any other obstacles. Hitting into them will slow you down and eat up your fuel.

Safe Landing: The only safe areas to land are the designated landing pads at the end of each level.

Look Out Below!: If you run out of jet packs, you will parachute safely to the ground. Depending on what level of the game you were in, you could end up anywhere on Club Penguin.

Fuel for Thought: Make sure to grab extra fuel as you fly to keep you going. Keep your eyes open for extra jet packs— if you catch one you'll get an extra life if you run out of fuel.

GAME TIP

If you complete the entire *Jet Pack Adventure* game without collecting a single coin along the way, you will get a bonus of 1,000 coins at the end!

Ship Ahoy: THE *MIGRATOR*

When Captain Rockhopper the pirate lands on Club Penguin, he docks at the Beach, behind the Lighthouse. You can always spot him in the telescope when he's on his way to the island.

Luckily for penguins everywhere, Rockhopper allows visitors onboard his ship when he's docked—this pirate prefers traveling alone. If you've visited the ship before, then you know that different parts of the *Migrator* have different names. Here's a little list of sailor lingo to help you find your way around:

Deck: This is the top floor of the ship, the part that stays above water. The deck is a great place for you and your friends to imagine you are pirates, sailing the seas. Recruit a crew and assign a part to everyone, including captain, first mate, navigator, and deckhands. Your captain can stand behind Rockhopper's steering wheel and lead you to a new, exciting destination.

Mast: This is the tall pole that holds up the ship's sails.

Jolly Roger: This is what a flag on a pirate ship is called. Rockhopper's jolly roger shows a white puffle and crossbones against a black background. You'll know the *Migrator* has been through stormy weather if the flag is tattered.

Crow's Nest: This is the small platform on top of the mast. You will often see Yarr, Rockhopper's puffle, bouncing up and down in the Crow's Nest. You and your navigator can climb the Crow's Nest and see what's on the horizon for your journey.

Hold: This area is below the decks. It's used to store ship supplies (like barrels of cream soda, Rockhopper's favorite drink). Rockhopper also keeps treasures here: items he finds on his journeys. When he docks his ship, he sells some of these items—and sometimes gives them away for free.

Captain's Quarters: "Quarters" is a sailing word that means the same thing as "bedroom." This room is where Rockhopper works and sleeps. For years Rockhopper kept the door

locked, but in April 2008 he gave penguins access to his quarters—if they could find the key. You still need the key to get into this space. It's hidden in the Book Room in Rockhopper's journal. Once you do get inside, you'll be rewarded with the chance to play a popular game: *Treasure Hunt*.

Save the *Migrator!*

It hasn't always been smooth sailing for Rockhopper and his pirate ship. In January 2008, the *Migrator* hit an iceberg and sank. Through the telescope, penguins spied Rockhopper and Yarr rowing to safety in a lifeboat, but the *Migrator* was lost beneath the ocean waves.

Penguins always help a friend in need, and the "Save the *Migrator*" campaign came about because everyone wanted to help Rockhopper. Working together with their friends, penguins had to find undersea wreckage, build a submarine to recover the pieces, and begin reconstruction of the ship.

Working around the clock, the *Migrator* was put back together in April 2008. Penguins set off flares at the Beach to signal Rockhopper, and when he and Yarr landed there was a huge celebration.

Treasure Hunt

Penguins who saw Rockhopper's quarters for the first time were excited to find this game waiting for them. To play this game, you need a friend. The key to success is cooperation.

Dig It: The game takes place in a box of sand. You and your friend take turns digging up squares of sand in the box. If you dig in the right spot, you will uncover treasure!

Coins and Jewels: Red rubies are worth twenty-five coins, a gold dubloon is worth one, and the rare green emerald is worth one hundred. To earn your reward, you have to uncover each coin or jewel completely.

Work Together: If your friend digs up a piece of a jewel, make sure to dig next to that piece on your turn. It's the only way to get the treasure.

GAME TIP

Look for a sparkle underneath the sand. It's a clue that there may be a jewel or coin buried there.

AUNT ARCTIC SAYS

Captain Rockhopper is a dear old friend of mine. I enjoy reading about his exciting adventures on the notice board in his quarters. And I am quite fond of the parties he throws when he comes ashore. My favorite was the 2007 Fall Fair. Rockhopper brought a paddle game, a spinning wheel, a puffle feeding game, and my favorite—the Memory Game. Things always get more interesting on Club Penguin when Rockhopper visits us!

107

Meet Rockhopper

Occupation: Pirate captain

Where He Calls Home: The sea, although he is originally from Club Penguin. His other base is Rockhopper Island.

Best Friend: Yarr, his red puffle

Most Valued Possession: The *Migrator*

Most Memorable Discoveries:
- Finding the red puffles
- Rockhopper Island

Favorite Sayings:
- "Yarr!"
- "Ahoy!"
- "Avast!"

Most Outrageous Trait: He isn't happy unless he's braving the dangers of the ocean, looking for adventure.

How He Relaxes: He likes to unwind at the end of a busy day by writing about his journeys while enjoying a cream soda.

When He's Not Sailing You Can Find Him:
- Counting his treasure
- Playing tag with his mateys
- Dancing a jig
- Giving penguins a tour of his ship

Bet You Didn't Know: Rockhopper built the *Migrator* with his own bare flippers.

Meet Yarr

Occupation: First mate of the *Migrator*

Special Talent: Surfing the ocean waves

Favorite Way to Pass the Time on a Long Voyage: Shooting snowballs out of the cannon in the Crow's Nest

Bet You Didn't Know: Yarr got his name because he answered every time Rockhopper cried out, "Yarr!"

TIP

When Rockhopper is visiting Club Penguin, the best places to look for him are the *Migrator*, the Dock, and the Iceberg. If you find him and ask him to be your buddy, he will give you a signed photo of himself.

Rockhopper discovered red puffles on an adventure in 2006. The puffles liked Rockhopper so much they hopped onboard the *Migrator* and sailed with him to Club Penguin. Now you can adopt one at the Pet Shop!

DID YOU KNOW?

Rockhopper's Treasures

When Rockhopper finds treasure, he doesn't keep it all for himself. He brings a lot of it to Club Penguin with him and sells it from his ship. Sometimes, he even gives free items away. Here's a look at some of the things he's brought back from his travels.

Clothing:

- pirate's eye patch
- pirate's bandana
- pirate belt
- puffle bandana
- tricorn hat
- safari hat
- blue flippers
- admiral's hat
- alien antenna
- pirate shoes
- red pirate bandana
- pirate dress
- captain's coat
- sailor shirt
- blue mask and snorkel
- admiral's jacket
- monocle
- striped overalls
- red pirate dress
- striped sash dress
- winged helmet
- gray pirate coat

CREW

Furniture Items:

- treasure chest
- ship in a bottle
- porthole
- ancient penguin monument
- pirate ship
- waves
- flamingo
- potted plant
- ship steering wheel
- wall treasure map
- jolly roger flag

Other:

- stuffed parrot
- gold wristwatch
- seashell necklace

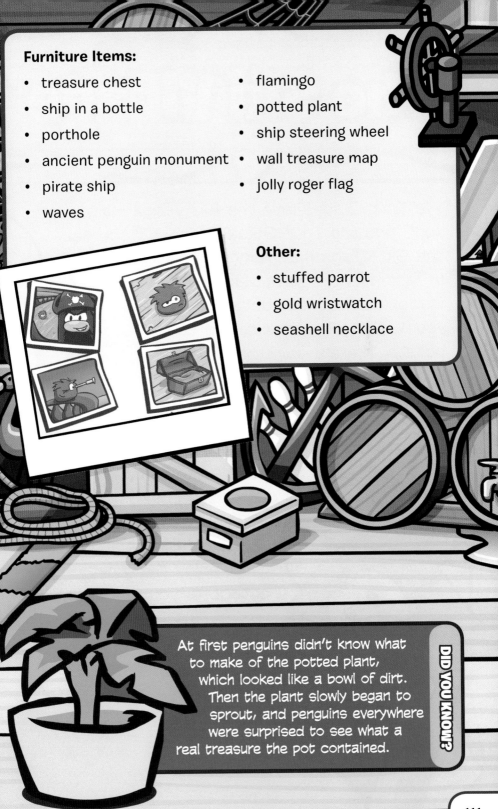

At first penguins didn't know what to make of the potted plant, which looked like a bowl of dirt. Then the plant slowly began to sprout, and penguins everywhere were surprised to see what a real treasure the pot contained.

DID YOU KNOW?

The Ski Village

"We Tour Guides love the Ski Village—it's where you'll find the Tour Guide booth. Of course, the Ski Village has many other attractions. In fact, it's the best place to find both indoor and outdoor activities. Whether you're a sports fanatic or a couch potato, there's something in the Ski Village for you.

"Feel like racing down a snowy slope? Then check out the Ski Hill. In the mood to catch some fish and earn some coins? Try some *Ice Fishing*. If you'd rather stay inside than enjoy the great outdoors, you can always chill in the Ski Lodge or go shopping in the Sport Shop."

Every day, new penguins waddle into Club Penguin. In the early days, these penguins had to find their way around the island without any help. But that all changed in 2007.

That's when Tour Guides appeared on the scene. These penguins play a very important role. They volunteer their time to give tours to new penguins. Tour Guides share the information they know about each place— everything from game tips, interesting facts, and advice about how to get around. Their question-mark hats are a welcome sight to penguins who might be lost or confused.

If you would like a tour, the most likely place to find a Guide is behind the booth. Approach the Tour Guide and ask for a tour. Be sure to stick close to your Guide as you waddle around the island. And when your tour is over, don't forget to say thank you!

TIP

To ask for a tour in Safe Chat mode, click on the speech bubble on your toolbar. Then scroll up to Questions and click on the one that reads, "Can I have a tour?"

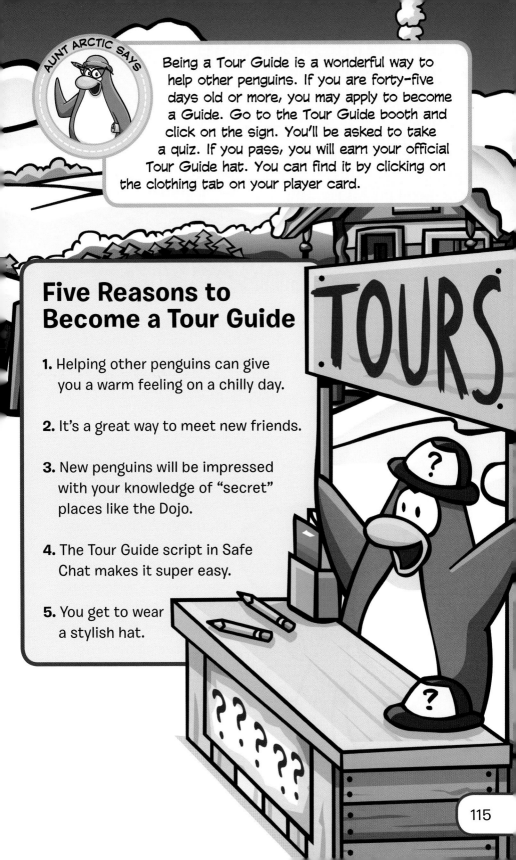

AUNT ARCTIC SAYS

Being a Tour Guide is a wonderful way to help other penguins. If you are forty-five days old or more, you may apply to become a Guide. Go to the Tour Guide booth and click on the sign. You'll be asked to take a quiz. If you pass, you will earn your official Tour Guide hat. You can find it by clicking on the clothing tab on your player card.

Five Reasons to Become a Tour Guide

1. Helping other penguins can give you a warm feeling on a chilly day.

2. It's a great way to meet new friends.

3. New penguins will be impressed with your knowledge of "secret" places like the Dojo.

4. The Tour Guide script in Safe Chat makes it super easy.

5. You get to wear a stylish hat.

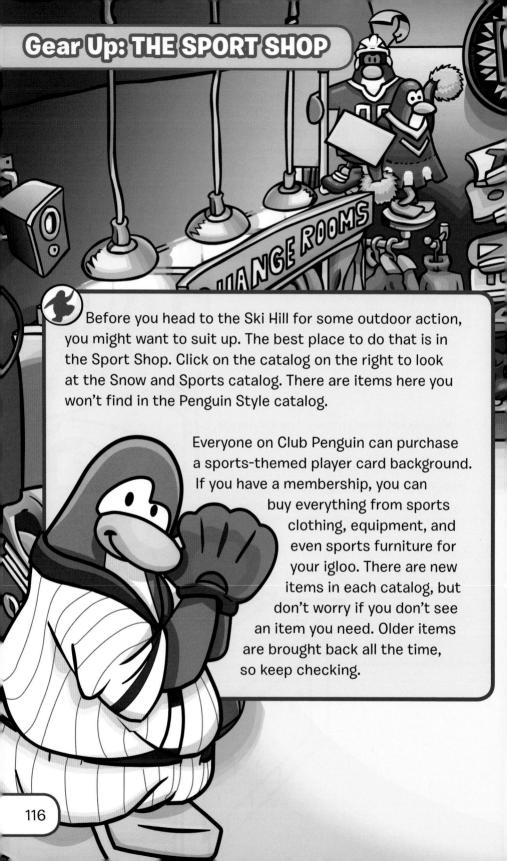

Gear Up: THE SPORT SHOP

Before you head to the Ski Hill for some outdoor action, you might want to suit up. The best place to do that is in the Sport Shop. Click on the catalog on the right to look at the Snow and Sports catalog. There are items here you won't find in the Penguin Style catalog.

Everyone on Club Penguin can purchase a sports-themed player card background. If you have a membership, you can buy everything from sports clothing, equipment, and even sports furniture for your igloo. There are new items in each catalog, but don't worry if you don't see an item you need. Older items are brought back all the time, so keep checking.

Here are just some of the things sports fans can expect to find in the catalog:

Football Fans: Helmets and red and blue jerseys

Hockey Fans: Sticks, helmets, and red and blue jerseys

Soccer Fans: Red and blue jerseys

Baseball Fans: Baseball glove, red and blue uniforms, red and blue baseball caps

Fishing Fans: Hats, fishing rods

Referees: Striped referee shirt

Cheerleaders: Red and blue cheerleading uniforms

Surfers: Flame Surfboard, Daisy Surfboard

Boogie Boarders: Pink striped wakeboard, yellow arrow wakeboard

Other Equipment: Tennis racket, treadmill, gym mats, exercise ball, exercise bike

The items in the catalog are more than just a way to look good. You and your friends can buy matching uniforms and form your own team. Put on a cheerleading uniform and waddle around, giving a cheer to every penguin you meet. What else can you do with the items in the Snow and Sports catalog? Why not put something on and try it out!

Join the Rescue Squad!

You may find a rescue squad uniform in the pages of the catalog. Penguins who wear this uniform are doing more than making a fashion statement—they're helping to keep Club Penguin safe.

Rescue Squad teams began by patrolling the Ski Hill, and then the squads appeared all over the island, ready to spring into action if a natural disaster strikes. If a Rescue Squad penguin warns you that an earthquake or storm is coming, follow them to a safe place.

If you're anxious for some winter sports action, hop on the Ski Lift to be carried to the top of the Ski Hill. The Ski Hill has one of the best views on Club Penguin. But the main reason penguins come here is to have sled races against one another. If you're feeling adventurous, join one of the races. If the Ski Hill is empty, send a "Sled Race" postcard to a buddy who's online at the same time as you, and ask them to join you for a race. Sled Racing is a great way to make new friends, so don't be shy—ask a penguin you meet to join you for a race.

AUNT ARCTIC SAYS

Every Snow and Sports catalog has a secret item hidden inside. Move your mouse over the items in the catalog until a little hand appears, and then click to reveal the item. You may have heard about a secret silver surfboard in the catalog. Finding that item is a little trickier: On the surfboard page, click on the surfboard that the penguin is holding. Then click on the starfish and then the clamshell for the chance to buy the silver surfboard.

EXPRESS

Sled Racing

Whether you're in the mood for an easy glide or feel like sliding at super speed, there's a Sled Race for you!

How to Play:

Find a Race: Walk to one of the sled runs. The Bunny Hill is the easiest run and the best way to learn the game. Ridge Run is the most difficult and has the most sleds. When you make your choice, a screen will appear that asks if you want to play. Click "yes." The race can't begin until enough penguins join in.

Don't Wipe Out: Once the race has begun, use your arrow keys to move left and right as you speed down the hill. Use the arrow keys to avoid obstacles such as a log or a tree branch. If you hit one, you will wipe out. But you'll quickly get back on your snow tube and continue racing.

Finish First: The race ends when all penguins cross the finish line. You will earn coins depending on how you place in the race.

GAME TIP

Slide over an ice patch to go extra fast!

MULLET

After a day of playing winter sports, there's nothing like relaxing in front of a warm fire. You'll find one inside the Ski Lodge. This rustic log cabin is filled with comfy couches and some interesting wall hangings, including a large moose head and a cuckoo clock. Playing a few games of *Find Four* at one of the tables here is a pleasant way to pass the time. You can also head out the back door for some *Ice Fishing*. You can earn coins by catching fish. And if you're lucky, you may even catch the legendary big fish, the Mullet!

The Ski Lodge has two floors, so climb up the ladder to the Lodge Attic. There are more *Find Four* games up there. Like many attics, the Lodge Attic sometimes holds some unusual surprises. After the big snowstorm of 2006, the extra snow was stored in the Lodge Attic and then used for the Festival of Snow in 2007. And in December 2007, the top of the large Christmas tree in the Ski Lodge extended all the way into the Lodge Attic. Who knows what will find its way into the Lodge Attic next?

123

Find Four

Looking for something to do with your buddy? Why not play a game of *Find Four*? Once you learn the rules, it's easy to master.

How to Play:

Find a Partner: Walk to a game table to challenge a player who's sitting there, or wait for someone to challenge you.

GAME TIP

Find Four is a game of strategy, not speed! Before you make a move, think about how you can win *and* block another player from winning at the same time.

Get Four in a Row: The object of the game is to be the first player to stack four round game pieces of the same color in a row: either up and down, across, or diagonally. When the game starts, your name will be highlighted when it is your turn to play. Click on the slot that you would like to drop your piece in. You and your opponent will take turns until one of you gets four pieces in a row.

ICE FISHING

This slow-paced game is great for beginners, and it's a nice way to relax and earn coins at the same time. To play, head for the door marked "Gone Fishing" in the back of the Ski Lodge.

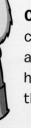

Catch Fish!: You must have a worm on your hook to catch a fish. Move your mouse up and down to raise and lower your hook. When you see a fish, lower your hook to the fish and catch it. Raise your hook above the ice and click your mouse to release the fish.

Steer Clear of Obstacles: Barrels and boots can kick fish off of your fishing line. Jellyfish, sharks, and crabs will cost you a worm if they touch your line.

Hold On to Your Worms: If you lose a worm, raise your hook above the water level and click on the can of worms to get a new one. You will begin the game with three worms. Once you lose all of them, the game is over. There's good news, though. You can catch a can of worms to get an extra life.

Collect Your Coins: At the end of the game, you will receive one coin for every fish you catch. If you catch the extra-big orange Mullet at the end, you will get an extra fifty coins.

Many penguins are puzzled about how to capture the Mullet at the end of the game. Here is some advice: This big fish needs bigger bait than a worm! After you first spot the Mullet approaching, three fish will pass by. One will swim near the top of the water, one will swim near the middle, and the third will swim near the bottom. Catch the first two fish and add them to your pile. Then catch the third fish, but don't release it! Let it hang there. Wiggle it around. Then see what happens . . .

Hidden Places

"No tour would be complete without showing you some of Club Penguin's hardest-to-find spots. These are places you can't easily find on the map, but they are worth visiting. Come along with me and we'll travel offshore to visit a popular party spot, then head deep into the mountains to find the hidden Dojo. Our last stop will be the Secret Agent Headquarters. We'll need special security clearance to get in there. When you're done touring these special places, you'll be able to impress your buddies with how well you know them."

Party Central: THE ICEBERG

HOW IT'S DONE

Want to jackhammer the Iceberg? You need a construction or miner's helmet. These are given away when construction sites pop up. If you have a membership, you can sometimes purchase them in the Penguin Style catalog. Wear it and nothing else. Then perform the "dance" action and drill away!

You're hanging out in town when penguins start spreading the word: "Party at the Iceberg!" Curious, you head to the Iceberg and find a crowd of penguins there, dancing and talking. Some are even wearing hard hats or mining helmets and using jackhammers to break into the ice! What's it all about?

The Iceberg is one of the most popular party spots on Club Penguin. With no furniture or buildings to get in the way, a whole lot of penguins can gather there and move around easily. But first, you have to get there. The Iceberg's location is a secret, unless you know where to look. Click on the map. On the right, you will see the Iceberg floating in the water. It's not marked. Click on it to go there.

Parties usually start when one or more penguin buddies go around the island, spreading the word. More and more penguins gather there until the Iceberg looks like it might sink.

That's the reason for those penguins using jackhammers. Shortly after the Iceberg parties started, rumors began to fly that the Iceberg could be tipped into the ocean if enough penguins crowded on one side of it. Then when the mining helmets were given away in May 2006, penguins thought drilling through the ice might work. The rumors keep on flying, but so far the Iceberg has never sunk. Still, it's fun to try.

In February 2008, the usually calm waters around the Iceberg became home to the *Aqua Grabber*. This underwater machine, invented by Gary the Gadget Guy, was built to help retrieve pieces of Captain Rockhopper's pirate ship, the *Migrator*, from the ocean floor.

AQUA GRABBER

GAME TIP

To clear the first level, you'll need to defeat a special clam and steal its giant pearl. Try to trick the clam by switching the pearl with a rock that's the same size and shape.

AUNT ARCTIC SAYS

My favorite games are the ones I can play with my puffles. If you have a pink puffle, take it for a walk, and then play *Aqua Grabber*. Your puffle will appear next to you in the game wearing scuba gear!

Explore the ocean depths by climbing in and taking the controls of the *Aqua Grabber*. You can pilot this marvelous piece of machinery as you hunt for treasure, encounter sea creatures, and even help clean up an underwater cream-soda spill.

How to Play:

Move Around: Use your arrow keys to move up, down, left, and right, and use the space bar to operate the grabber's claw and to drop and pick things up. Be careful not to bump into things, or you'll run out of air more quickly. You'll be searching for pearls, treasure chests, and soda barrels.

Grab the Goods: Each blue oyster contains a pearl. Wait until the oyster falls asleep before snatching the pearl.

Net Your Treasure: Small items can fit right on the *Aqua Grabber*, but if you grab big items, like a treasure chest, you need to bring it to the net. Be careful—if you bump into something, you'll drop what you're carrying.

Get Some Air!: If you run out of air, you will be ejected from the capsule and shot to the surface so you can breathe. Look for large air bubbles you can move over to fill up with extra oxygen. Large bubbles flow out of a vent on the ocean floor. You can also get air by going above the surface of the water.

Anyone can go to the Dojo—if you know the secret. To get there, click on the map on the bottom left of your screen. You won't see the Dojo the way you see other locations. You have to search for it. Move your cursor over the mountains to the right of the Ski Village. When a little hand icon appears, click, and you'll find yourself inside the Dojo.

A sunny room with high ceilings, the Dojo has windows on all the walls that let in lots of light. The floor is big and bare, with lots of room to run around. The only furniture to be found is two benches on either side of the room.

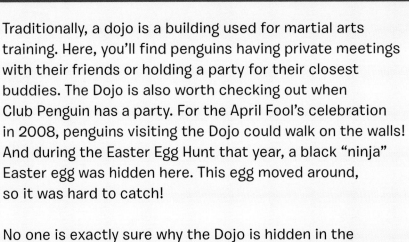

Traditionally, a dojo is a building used for martial arts training. Here, you'll find penguins having private meetings with their friends or holding a party for their closest buddies. The Dojo is also worth checking out when Club Penguin has a party. For the April Fool's celebration in 2008, penguins visiting the Dojo could walk on the walls! And during the Easter Egg Hunt that year, a black "ninja" Easter egg was hidden here. This egg moved around, so it was hard to catch!

No one is exactly sure why the Dojo is hidden in the mountains. That's one secret that may never be revealed.

Undercover:
SECRET AGENT HEADQUARTERS

What makes Club Penguin such a safe place? One of the reasons is the hard work of penguins who tirelessly patrol the island and help other penguins in distress. They are secret agents, a select group who make up the PSA (Penguin Secret Agency), with a lot of knowledge about the island. They work undercover and never reveal their identity. That penguin dancing with her puffle in the Night Club? She might be a secret agent. So could the penguin tossing pizza in the Pizza Parlor, or the one telling jokes at The Stage.

It all happens at Secret Agent Headquarters, the secret hub of the island. Only secret agents are allowed inside HQ (Headquarters). The room has an entire wall of twenty-four monitors that show each room on Club Penguin. If there is trouble anywhere, a secret agent is immediately dispatched to solve the problem.

To get to HQ, a secret agent can teleport using the #102405 Spy Phone, a high-tech piece of equipment that every agent gets. Or they can use the secret entrance in the Sport Shop. It's the dressing room closest to the shop's front door.

Secret agents are always on duty. If they are partying with their buddies on the Iceberg, they still have to work. If they notice other penguins using bad language or harassing other penguins, the agents must report them to the moderator.

The more risky assignments are given out in HQ. Inside the room is a document called Case Files. It's a list of secret agent missions. Missions can be anything from testing Gary the Gadget Guy's latest inventions to searching for missing puffles. Agents must battle the elements and use both their brains and creativity to get the job done.

In order to succeed at missions, agents need to read "The F.I.S.H." F.I.S.H. stands for Factual Informative Spy Handbook and it's got everything an agent needs to know, including cool clothes and items for players with a membership to purchase, and a secret code that is needed in order to complete missions.

Secret agent missions can be tricky, but there is always a reward once you finish them. Of course, the best reward is knowing that Club Penguin is a better place!

AUNT ARCTIC SAYS

Becoming a secret agent is a big deal—you need lots of experience exploring Club Penguin. If you are thirty days old or more, click on the Moderator shield on the upper right of your screen. Then click on "Become a Secret Agent" to get started.

WANTED

Herbert P. Bear, Esq., and
his accomplice, Klutzy

for trying to disturb the peace.
Incidents include attempts to
chop down the Ski Lodge, stealing
coins from the Gift Shop,
and causing an earthquake.

Herbert is clawed and
possibly dangerous.

Secret Agents:
Know Your Spy Phone

Your spy phone has a long-range antenna that allows you to keep in touch with HQ no matter where you are on Club Penguin. Below the antenna and to the right you'll see an LED blinking light. Click on the light to reveal your spy tools. They can be really useful when you're on a secret agent mission.

Below the light is a viewscreen. You can click on the screen to change the room names, or use the scroll button on the left to change them. Once you see the name of the room you want to visit, click the "Teleport" button and you'll be taken there immediately.

Below the Teleport button is a button labeled "Visit HQ." Click on this button anytime for a direct link to Secret Agent Headquarters.

SUPERFLPPERB

Teleport

Visit HQ

EST CHAMBER

PLACE

Mission Impossible?

Even the smartest secret agents can get stuck trying to figure out how to complete the missions successfully. These tips can help you breeze through your missions with a bit more ease.

1. In some missions you can click on the map on the upper left of your screen to get around Club Penguin. Places marked with an *X* are places important to your mission.

2. Keep your eyes out for messages written in the secret agent code. You will always find the code bar on the bottom of your screen for easy decoding.

3. Remember that you have tools in your spy phone. If something needs to be moved or fixed, try using one of the tools on it. Click on the tool and then use your mouse to move it over an object. Click again to put it back in your inventory. If the tool doesn't work, you won't lose it—it will go right back in your inventory.

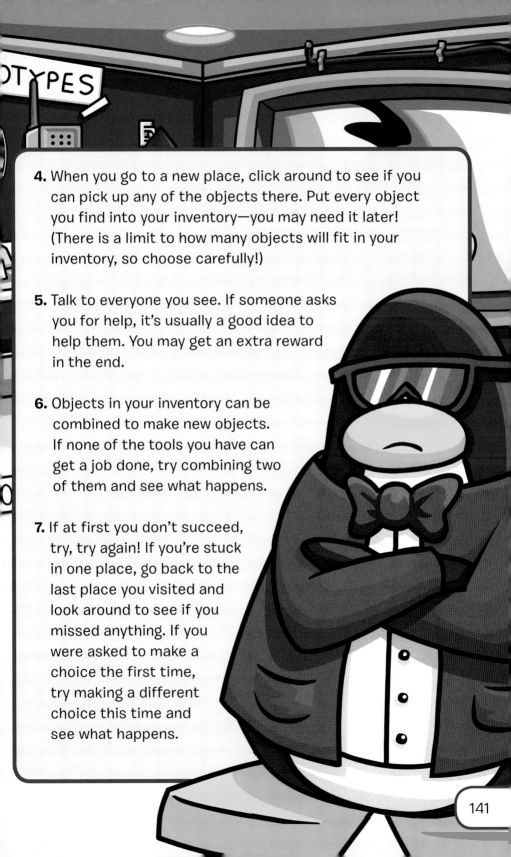

4. When you go to a new place, click around to see if you can pick up any of the objects there. Put every object you find into your inventory—you may need it later! (There is a limit to how many objects will fit in your inventory, so choose carefully!)

5. Talk to everyone you see. If someone asks you for help, it's usually a good idea to help them. You may get an extra reward in the end.

6. Objects in your inventory can be combined to make new objects. If none of the tools you have can get a job done, try combining two of them and see what happens.

7. If at first you don't succeed, try, try again! If you're stuck in one place, go back to the last place you visited and look around to see if you missed anything. If you were asked to make a choice the first time, try making a different choice this time and see what happens.

Meet Gary the Gadget Guy

Gary's Greatest Inventions

Here's a list of some of Gary's most important inventions. Nobody knows what Gary will invent next, so keep playing Club Penguin to see his latest creation. When Gary comes up with something new, you can usually read about it in *The Club Penguin Times*.

March 2006: spy phone
November 2006: *Jet Pack Adventure*
January 2007: AC 3000 cooling system
February 2007: *Pizzatron 3000*, snowball-powered clock
January 2008: *Crab Translator 3000*
February 2008: *Aqua Grabber*

Spotted in Gary's Gadget Room: Thingamajig 3000, life-preserver shooter, night-vision goggles, robotic penguin, prototype sled

Occupation: Gary is Club Penguin's resident inventor. He also has a secret identity when he works for the Penguin Secret Agency. Known simply as "G," he helps secret agents with missions and equips them with the latest spy gear.

Favorite Food: Pizza (it's why he invented the Pizzatron 3000)

Favorite Beverage: Coffee. It helps him stay up late to work on his inventions.

Most Memorable Inventions: The jet pack, Pizzatron 3000, Aqua Grabber . . . actually, they are all pretty memorable!

His Favorite Thing about His Job: As an inventor, Gary enjoys coming to the rescue with one of his inventions whenever there is an emergency. As "G," he is proud to work with secret agents to help keep Club Penguin a safe place.

When He's Not Working You Can Find Him: Reading unusual scientific facts

All Work and No Party?: Don't worry about Gary. He found time to party at the 2008 Medieval Party—he even got dressed up like a knight!

He Never Leaves Home Without: A notebook and a pen. He always writes ideas down so he won't forget them.

Bet You Didn't Know: Gary's workshop is located along the back wall of the Sport Shop.

Hiding Places

Ready for a game of hide-and-seek? There are a few places on Club Penguin where you can hide and see other penguins but they won't know you are there.

Waddle over to the Pizza Parlor and head to the pizza oven. Some sacks of flour are stacked up in the corner on the floor. Stand behind them and you'll become invisible. You can do the same in the Mine Shack if you go behind the icy stalagmite on the lower right of the screen.

Now that you know the best hiding spots, go ahead and challenge your friends to a game of hide-and-seek. Maybe you'll discover even more great hiding places!

Igloo

"Home sweet igloo! Let's take a look at the places that every penguin on the island calls home. Your igloo is a great place to meet quietly with a friend, or have a party with a bunch of buddies. You can even open up your igloo to the whole island, so any penguin who wants to can drop by and say hi.

"If you have a membership, you can use coins to transform your igloo into a place that really shows your personality. In this section you'll find out all the possible ways you can decorate your igloo—and get great tips on how to turn your igloo into the hottest spot on Club Penguin!"

Start Shopping

If you have a membership, you can decorate your igloo any way you want. The first thing you'll need is coins—lots of them—so you can purchase items you need from catalogs. You won't find these catalogs in any store. They're right inside your igloo so you can shop from the comfort of your own home.

Go to your igloo by clicking on the house-shaped icon in the toolbar on the bottom of your screen. See that measuring-tape icon on the right? Click on it. A bunch of new icons will appear. Check out the one shaped like an igloo, and the one that looks like a blue catalog.

Click on the blue catalog to open up the Better Igloos catalog. A new catalog is published every two months. Inside, you'll find everything you need to trick out your space: furniture, electronics equipment, pictures and posters for the walls, rugs for the floor, and other accessories. When you buy an item, it goes inside the storage box on the right of your screen.

CHECK **IT** OUT

If you see an item you want but can't afford it, be patient. Items in the Better Igloos catalog often go on sale. You might be able to buy what you want at a low, low price!

The Better Igloos catalog is great for decorating, but if you want an extreme igloo makeover, click on the igloo icon. This will reveal the Igloo Upgrades catalog. If you've saved up enough coins, you can change your igloo design. Want more color? Then an igloo with blue or pink walls is perfect for you. Need more space? Try a duplex with two floors. In the mood for some fantasy? You might be more comfortable in a castle igloo. There are several igloo styles to choose from, and there are always new ones being added.

Another way to upgrade your igloo is to add a new floor. A green rug feels nice and soft under flippered feet. If you love a good dance party, then a wall-to-wall dance floor might be what you need. Easy-to-clean linoleum is a great choice if you've got a pad full of puffles. And if you don't like your new floor, it's easy to get rid of. Just pay twenty coins for Floor Removal Service, available inside the catalog.

AUNT ARCTIC SAYS

The Better Igloos catalog always has a secret item hidden inside. To find it, move your mouse around all of the objects you see until a little hand appears. Then click.

DID YOU KNOW?

When you upgrade your igloo, all your furniture and stuff gets put back in storage. So don't panic when you see your new igloo and it looks empty! Click open the storage box, and you'll find everything there.

Decorate Your Igloo

After you buy an item, you can move it from your storage box to your igloo. To do this, make sure you're in edit mode by clicking on the tape measure on the right. Then click on the storage box. The items in the box are arranged by category: furniture, stuff that hangs on walls, and stuff that covers the floor. Click on the inventory tab to move between the categories.

To drop an item in the room, click on it. Move your mouse to the spot where you want it and click again. The item will appear in your igloo. If you don't like where you put it, just keep clicking on it and moving it until you're happy. You can do this as long as you're in edit mode. When you leave edit mode, you can't move your furniture around.

Once you like where an item is, you can rotate it so it faces a different way. To do this, press on the left and right arrows on your keyboard. When you're satisfied, stop. When you're done with all of your decorating, click on the measuring tape to exit edit mode. Now everything will stay exactly as you want it—until you get the urge to redecorate again!

DID YOU KNOW? When you buy items for your puffle in the Pet Shop, they will go into your storage box. Go into your igloo, click on the measuring tape, and then click on the storage box to place these items in your igloo.

TIP

Be sure to leave edit mode when you're done decorating by clicking on the measuring tape.

Some items, such as electronic equipment, have cool features that you can play around with. When you're in edit mode, click on an item and press the up and down arrow keys on your keyboard to see if anything happens. If you have a television set, doing this will change the channels. This will also light a fire in your fireplace, or open up your refrigerator. Experiment to see what else your stuff can do.

If you are tired of an item, or want to keep it in storage for a while, just click on it and use your mouse to drag it back into the storage box. The item will stay in storage until you need it again.

Now you know what to do to decorate your igloo. But how should your igloo look? There are as many ways to decorate your igloo as there are penguins on the island. The choice is completely up to you!

Awesome Igloo Items

These popular items can be found in igloos all over
Club Penguin. If you don't see them in the current catalog,
don't worry. There's a good chance they'll pop up in
a future catalog.

Party Banner: One or more of
these sets the stage for any
festive get-together.

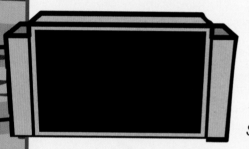

LCD Television: More
affordable than the big screen
TV, this set allows penguins
to watch their favorite shows,
from the weather report to
Sled Racing.

Balloons: They're cheap to buy, and having a few of them
in your igloo practically screams, "Instant party!"

Home Stereo and Speakers: Fill your igloo
with speakers to get that Night
Club sound and feel.

Orange Inflatable Sofa: This soft, bouncy sofa adds a bright pop of color to your pad.

Puffle Bed: A cozy place for puffles to curl up and sleep, available in the Love Your Pet catalog. Some puffle owners purchase one bed for each puffle.

Snowman: Penguins love snow, and this cheerful snowman is a great way to bring the outdoors inside.

Fireplace: There's nothing like a blazing fire to warm up a chilly penguin on a winter night.

Tiki Torch: Station two of these above your doorway so your guests can make a dramatic entrance!

Refrigerator: Sure, it's cold inside your igloo, but a refrigerator is a stylish and practical way to store your favorite foods.

Super Styles

In every Better Igloos catalog, you'll find furniture grouped together to form a theme. Don't be disappointed if you can't find this stuff in the catalog you're looking at. Club Penguin loves to bring back old favorites!

Sports Fan's Hangout

In this well-equipped space, sports-loving penguins can get ready for the arena by working out on the gym machines, or they can invite some buddies over to watch the game on TV.

Underwater Paradise

Are you a mermaid at heart? Then you'll be right at home in this hideaway under the waves, complete with a giant clam!

Cool Castle

Feel like a king or queen in this royal pad.
Invite your buddies over for a party—it'll be sure
to be a *knight* they'll remember!

Halloween Haven

This jack-o'-lantern igloo is a creepy yet comfortable
home for penguins who love this spooky holiday. If
you live in this pumpkin and some penguins knock on
the door, make sure to give them treats—not tricks!

Extreme Igloos

In your travels around Club Penguin, you may see some igloos that make you go, "Wow! How'd they do that?" The answer is, of course, lots of coins—but even more than that, creativity. Check out other penguins' extreme igloo styles. Maybe they'll inspire you to create an extreme igloo of your own!

Dancer's Delight

Early catalogs offered a small dance floor that could be placed inside an igloo. Many penguins bought lots of dance floors and covered their entire igloos with them to make their own personal dance hall. In May 2007, Club Penguin started to offer a Dance Floor option in the Igloo Upgrades catalog, so you can cover your space with one easy step.

Pufflemaniacs

Some puffle owners devote their entire igloo space to their special pets. They raid the Love Your Pet furniture catalog for pet beds, igloos, scratching towers, pet dishes, and more. There is barely room for a penguin to waddle in these puffle palaces!

A few times a year, Club Penguin holds igloo-decorating contests. You can find out about them by reading the newspaper.

CHECK IT OUT

The Big Stack

Some puffle owners turn their igloos into works of art by stacking things on top of one another until the whole igloo is filled up. Stacking television sets is a popular pastime.

Thinking Outside the Box

Some penguins look at one thing and think, "I can do something else with that!" They line up bookcases in a row to make walls. They put a bunch of puffle beds together to make one big bed. Use your arrow keys and your imagination to make something new with what you already have!

Now you've seen how some penguins have created extreme igloos. What can you do with your igloo? Turn it into a restaurant or a library? Make it into something spectacular to look at? The choice is up to you!

Party On!

There are many great party spots on Club Penguin, but sometimes the best place to party is in your own igloo! To start, you might want to decorate your igloo with banners, balloons, and lights from the Better Igloos catalog. The next thing you'll want is some party music.

To play music in your igloo, you'll need some kind of stereo or jukebox. You can buy this in the Better Igloos catalog. Take the stereo out of your storage box and drop it in your igloo. Then click on the cassette tape icon on the right. You will see a choice of music types. Click on each one to sample the music. When you find one you like, leave it on. This music will play every time you or someone else enters your igloo.

Now that your igloo is set, you'll need some guests. If you want to keep the party private, invite only penguins you know. You can send a postcard to penguins on your buddy list inviting them to your igloo.

If you want to invite penguins you don't know, you can open your igloo on the main map. To do this, go into your igloo. Click the *lock* icon on the right to unlock your igloo. Now when other penguins click on the igloo on the main map, they will see your name. By clicking on your name, they will be transported to your igloo. If you don't get a lot of guests at first, you can always go to Town Center and tell other penguins to come to your party on the map.

You can also use this method to visit other penguins' igloos. Click on the names of penguins who have open igloos to see who's having the best party.

Igloo Party Tips

If you're giving a party . . .

- Greet your guests when they come in. Some of your guests might by shy, so be sure to say hello or ask how they're doing.
- Give your guests something to do. Start to dance, or begin a friendly snowball fight.

If you're going to a party . . .

- Be sure to compliment your host's igloo using one of your emotes in the chat bar.
- Don't start a snowball fight unless your host starts one first.
- If you have to leave, say good-bye!

Join the Community

"Of course, Club Penguin is about much more than just games and coins. It's the penguins who live, play, and work here that make it such a special place. Whatever you and your buddies can dream up, you can make happen on Club Penguin. Do you want to have a pizza party at the Beach? Organize a search team to look for the latest pin? It's all about using your imagination. And what makes it so great is you get to share the fun with penguins from all different places.

"Becoming part of the community can be as easy as making a buddy or as involved as putting on a play at The Stage. You can contribute art, jokes, puzzles, and stories. In this section, you'll find these—and a bunch of ways—to get in on the action."

You've Got to Have Friends

You're hanging out in the Coffee Shop when suddenly you receive a buddy request. You click on the smiley-face postcard and see this message: "So-and-so wants to be your buddy. Do you accept?" What exactly does this mean? When you accept another penguin as your buddy, you will appear on each other's buddy list. When a penguin is on your buddy list, you can see if they're online, visit their igloo, and send them mail. It's a way to make sure you can find a friend again after you meet them.

You can ask another player to be your buddy, too. If you see a penguin you'd like to get to know better, click on them. Their player card will appear on your screen. Click on the yellow smiley face on the bottom of their player card. You will be asked if you want to ask that penguin to be your buddy. Choose "yes," or "no" if you've changed your mind. If the other penguin accepts, they will appear on your buddy list. You can have as many as 100 buddies!

You can access your buddy list by clicking on the smiley-face icon on the toolbar on the bottom of your screen. When you open it, you will see a list of your buddies. If there is a yellow smiley face next to the penguin's name, that means the penguin is in the same server as you. No matter where your buddy is, you can click on their name to see their player card. You can take several actions, depending on what you want to do:

 Remove Buddy: If you don't want to be buddies anymore, or want to make room for more buddies, simply click on this icon to remove them.

Find: Click this button to find out where your buddy is. Then go there and say hello!

 Visit Home: You can click this button to visit your friend's igloo, whether your friend is home or not.

 Send Mail: You can send mail to any of your buddies, no matter where they are. Click the envelope on the top of your screen to send mail to your buddies. Your list of buddies is the first page of the Penguin Mail postcard catalog. Scroll through the names until you find the one you want. Next, flip through the postcard catalog to find the one you want to send. You can even send mail to a friend who is not online—they'll be able to read it the next time they log in. If you want to reply to a postcard someone sent you, simply click the reply icon. If you want to delete a postcard, click the delete icon.

Would you like to send mail to a penguin you are not friends with yet? No problem. Click on the penguin to pull up his or her player card and click . You'll be buddies in no time!

Keep in mind that it costs coins to send mail—about ten coins per postcard.

 Report Player: If your buddy is using bad language or threatening you in any way, you can report him or her to the moderator. (This button appears on every player card, so you can report a player whether or not they are your buddy.)

You will be surprised how easy it is to make a lot of buddies. So, now that you have all of these buddies, what happens next? Don't worry—here are lots of great ideas for cool things you can do with your buddies.

How It's Done: Meet Your Friends Online

You probably have friends or brothers or sisters who love Club Penguin as much as you do. To become buddies with them, you have to find them on Club Penguin. Pick a server, and set a time and a place where you will all meet, like this, for example: Blizzard, 7:00, on the Iceberg. Once you are in the same place, you can click on one another and become buddies. After that, it will be easy to find each other when you're on Club Penguin!

Say What?

The best way to get to know your buddy is to talk to them. You can type in what you want to say using the toolbar on the bottom of your screen. Click on the speech bubble icon, and the words will appear in a speech bubble coming out of your mouth. This is called Safe Chat mode, because you're not able to type in bad words.

You can only use this feature if you are *not* set up for Ultimate Safe Chat mode. Luckily, every penguin can use the messages option on your toolbar to communicate. You can simply say "hello" or "good-bye." There are also answers to questions you might be asked, such as "Boy or girl?" You can even ask questions to other penguins, such as "Want to play?" or "Where did you find that pin?" To access these messages, click on the speech bubble all the way on the left of your toolbar. Then scroll up and over to see all the different choices there are. Click on the word or phrase you want to say.

I Feel 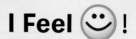!

When words can't express how you feel, say it with emotes! These little icons can show how you feel 😠 or help you ask for what you want 🌸. To access them, click on the winking smiley face on the left side of your toolbar. Then scroll up until you see the emote icon that you want, and click on it. It will appear in a speech bubble coming out of your mouth.

AUNT ARCTIC SAYS

Even though I am a writer, words sometimes can't express all I'm feeling when I'm spending time with my good friends. I've found the emotes really come in handy. In fact, I enjoy using them so much that I've discovered five secret emote shortcuts that do not appear on the official Club Penguin list. They are: ei (igloo); ep (puffle); em (coin); en (moon and stars). Hit et to get a musical note—with an extra sound! Try it and see what happens.

If scrolling takes too long, you can use these keyboard shortcuts to choose an emote. Just hit the keys to make the emote appear:

- e1 = Laughing face
- e2 = Smiley
- e3 = Straight face
- e4 = Frown
- e5 = Surprise
- e6 = Sticking out tongue
- e7 = Wink
- e8 = Green sick face
- e9 = Red angry face
- e0 = Sad face
- eu = Crooked face

- ec = Coffee cup
- eg = Game
- eo = Popcorn
- ez = Pizza
- eq = Ice cream
- ek = Cake
- el = Good luck
- eb = Lightbulb
- eh = Heart
- ef = Flower

Ten Things to Do with Your Buddies

1. Dress Alike: Put on the same color, clothes, hair, or more, and hang out somewhere together so everyone can see you're buddies!

2. Plan a Party: In advance, decide where and when your party will be. Tell your buddies, and tell them to tell *their* buddies. To keep it exclusive, give the party location in code, or come up with a riddle that penguins have to figure out.

Putting on a play

3. Put on a Play: Tell your friends to meet you at The Stage and perform the newest play there. (Not sure how to do it? Check out Section Four of this guide).

4. Surprise Snowball Fight: Head to the Snow Forts, or go to someplace unexpected, like the Coffee Shop. When the group leader gives the signal (like a lightbulb emote, for example), let the snowball fight begin!

5. Get Your Game On: Head to the Ice Rink to play the latest sport featured there. Or for some one-on-one gaming, play *mancala* or *Find Four* together.

6. Go Party Hopping: Go to every open igloo party together. Start with the first one on the list, and work your way down.

Playing music together

7. Have a Fashion Show: Set a time and place. You could do this in your igloo, at the Lighthouse, or even on The Stage. Invite penguins to come up one at a time in their best outfit. Penguins can rate the contestants on a scale of one to five.

8. Start a Band: Buy instruments in the Penguin Style catalog. Decide on a name for your band. Then head to the Lighthouse and jam on the small stage there. Make sure to tell other penguins the name of your band!

9. Try to Tip the Iceberg: Put on a hard hat or mining helmet, head to the Iceberg, perform the "dance" action, and start drilling! (Make sure you're not wearing other clothing items.) Sure, it hasn't worked yet—but it's still fun to try!

10. Party Like a Pirate: Put on your best pirate gear, give a cry of "Shiver me timbers!" and storm the Coffee Shop or the Pizza Parlor. (You can wear gear given away for free by Rockhopper. If you're a member, you can buy pirate gear in the Pirate catalog, usually found inside the *Migrator*.)

Club Penguin Parties

The Coffee Shop decorated for a party

In other sections, you've heard about igloo parties and Iceberg parties. These kinds of parties happen every day. But about once a month, Club Penguin throws official island-wide parties. These are celebrations you definitely don't want to miss!

At an official party, special decorations are set up all around the island. There are unusual decorations to see, new things to click on, and free items are given away. Sometimes special items appear in the Penguin Style or Better Igloos catalogs that match the theme of the party.

The party themes usually have to do with the time of year. You can count on some parties to happen annually, such as the Halloween Party, April Fool's Day Party, or Christmas Party. Other parties only happen once, such as the Underground Party, which was held to celebrate the opening of the Boiler Room and Cave.

In November 2007, penguins got a chance to vote on which special party they wanted to return. The winner was the Wild West Party, where every penguin can feel like a cowpoke for a few days. Yee-ha!

Scavenger Hunt!

From time to time, Club Penguin holds special scavenger hunts. Penguins are given clues that lead to the discovery of treasures or new places. The most popular scavenger hunt is the annual Easter Egg Hunt. Six eggs are hidden in different places around the island for penguins to find.

Club Penguin's Biggest Blowouts!

There's something new to do at every Club Penguin party. A few of the parties have been so amazing that penguins can't stop talking about them!

Christmas 2006: Every room in Club Penguin was decorated for the holiday. Colorful lights twinkled from the trees. Giant candy canes stuck out of snowbanks. A bright red bulb shone from the Beacon, and gingerbread cookies baked in the oven at this festive party.

Christmas 2006

Fall Fair 2007: Maybe the most extreme Club Penguin party ever, thanks to Captain Rockhopper. The pirate brought six new games to play at the party, including *Puffle Shuffle*, *Ring the Bell* (a test of strength), and *Grab and Spin*, a wheel of chance. Penguins played games to earn tickets, and then traded in those tickets for cool prizes.

Halloween 2007

Halloween 2007: The highlight of this party was an island-wide candy hunt. Penguins started by finding a pumpkin basket to hold their candy, then solved clues to find the location of eight pieces of candy. Penguins who found all eight pieces won a prize.

Water Party 2007: All of Club Penguin was turned into an underwater paradise for this party, held when the Underground flooded. The dance floor at the Night Club was blue, and water shot out of it to spray the dancers. Penguins could take a dip in the blowup pool in the Coffee Shop and grab a burger at the hut on the Beach. The Snow Forts were replaced with a giant inflatable octopus and squid. Today, you can still find penguins wearing the umbrella hats that were given away for free at this bash.

Water Party 2007

Free Items

Did you ever see a penguin roasting a marshmallow on a stick, or hovering around with a propeller beanie, and wonder where they got that cool item? These are just some examples of items that are given away for free at official parties. The items are usually only available while the party is on, but don't worry—sometimes they're offered again when the next party rolls around.

Here's a look at some free party items you might have missed:

Anniversary Items
Club Penguin opened in October 2005. The very first party was a Beta party to celebrate the first time Club Penguin opened its doors to penguins all over the world. Every October, Club Penguin celebrates its anniversary with a party.

- Beta hat (October 2005)
- One-year party hat (October 2006)
- Two-year party hat (October 2007)

Halloween Items
- Wizard hat (October 2006)
- Pumpkin basket (October 2007)
- Halloween scarf (October 2007)

Christmas Items
- Santa hat (December 2005, December 2006, December 2007)
- Christmas scarf (December 2005, December 2007)
- Santa beard (December 2006)
- Reindeer antlers (December 2007)

Winter Luau Item
- Red and orange lei (January 2006)

Winter Fiesta Items
- Maracas—Dance while holding this item to shake your maracas. (January 2007)

Festival of Snow Items
- Snowflake shirt (February 2007)
- Ice crown (February 2007)

Valentine's Day Items
- Red tie (February 2006)
- Red sunglasses (February 2006)
- Blue sunglasses (February 2006)

St. Patrick's Day Items
- Shamrock hat (March 2006)
- Really big shamrock hat (March 2008)

April Fool's Day Items
- Propeller cap—Dance while wearing this item, and you will hover in the air! (April 2006, April 2008)
- Funny nose glasses (April 2007)
- Swirly glasses (April 2008)

Easter Items
- Pink bunny ears (April 2006)
- Blue bunny ears (April 2007)
- Green bunny ears (April 2008)

Underground Items
- Mining helmet—Dance while wearing this item, and you will use a jackhammer. (May 2006)

Summer Items

- Inflatable duck—Dance while wearing this item, and you will swim. (June 2006)
- Water wings—You can swim if you dance while wearing these, too. (June 2006)
- Blue lei—Dance while wearing this item, and you will do the hula. (June 2006)
- Whistle—Wave while wearing this item, and hear the whistle blow! (June 2006)
- Ice cream apron—Dance while wearing this item to scoop out some ice cream. (June 2007)
- Flower headdress (June 2007)
- Green sunglasses (June 2007)
- Green inflatable duck—Dance while wearing this item, and you will swim. (June 2007)

Wild West Items

- Cowboy bandana (July 2006)

Sports Items

- Red face paint—Dance while wearing this item, and you will hold up a sign that reads, "Go Red!" (August 2006)
- Blue face paint—Dance while wearing this item, and you will hold up a sign that reads, "Go Blue!" (August 2006)
- Ice skates (August 2006)

Lighthouse Items
- Lighthouse shirt (September 2006)
- Red beanie (September 2006)

Pirate Party Item
- Sailor hat (May 2007)

Water Party Items
- Umbrella hat (July 2007)
- Blue water wings—Dance while wearing this item and your penguin will swim. (July 2007)

Camping Party Item
- Marshmallow on a stick (August 2007)

Fall Fair Items
- Feathered tiara (September 2007)
- Candy necklace (September 2007)
- Cotton candy (September 2007)
- Lollipop (September 2007)
- Paddle ball—Wave while wearing this item to hit the ball with the paddle. (September 2007)

Submarine Party Items
- Yellow snorkel (February 2008)
- Seashell belt (February 2008)

Medieval Party Items
- Square tunic (May 2008)

TIP

When you receive a free item, try dancing or waving with the item on and see what happens. Remember, don't wear anything else except that item.

Club Penguin Needs You!

Belonging to the Club Penguin community isn't just about parties and buddies. There are many ways you can pitch in to make Club Penguin a fun place for everyone who visits. There are things you can do every week, and some special opportunities that happen once in a while. The best way to find out how you can participate in these activities is to read *The Club Penguin Times* every week, or check the "What's New" feature. You can get to it by clicking on the yellow or orange penguin on the home page. Just click on "What's New" on the top left part of your screen.

Here's a look at some cool things penguins have done—and things you can do right now!

Contribute to *The Club Penguin Times*: The newspaper needs reporters to write articles, and to submit other things, too, such as tips, jokes, riddles, poetry, and comic strips. New submissions are published every week. Look in the last pages of the newspaper to find out how you can show off your talents to everyone on Club Penguin!

Enter Contests: Club Penguin's contests are designed to let a penguin's creativity shine. In February 2007, penguins designed ice sculptures, submitting their drawings to Club Penguin. The winning sculptures were on display at the Festival of Snow, a special Club Penguin party. During the annual Igloo Decorating Contest, penguins decorate their igloos in holiday finery, and pictures of the best ones are posted in the newspaper.

Take the Penguin Poll: Share your opinion about Club Penguin! Answer questions about Club Penguin in a poll and see what others think, too. To get to the poll, click on "Community" at clubpenguin.com.

Be a Tour Guide: If you are more than forty-five days old, you can take a test to become a Tour Guide. Just go to the Tour Guide booth in the Plaza. Once you earn your hat and sign, take some time once in a while to help new penguins around the island. (See page 114 for more info.)

Be a Secret Agent: If you are more than thirty days old, you can take the test to become a secret agent. Agents help keep Club Penguin safe by reporting penguins who use bad language to the moderator. (See page 136 for more info.)

Coins for Change: In December 2007, Club Penguin launched the Coins for Change program. For ten days, penguins all over the island were invited to donate their coins to one of three different charitable causes. More than two billion coins were donated. Then Club Penguin donated one million dollars in real dollars to the charities, dividing up the money based on how many coins were donated to each one. Penguins everywhere felt good about helping to make a difference!

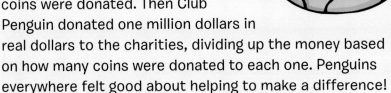

As you can see, there are lots you can do to be active in the Club Penguin community. There's always something new and exciting going on, so be on the lookout for the latest ways to get involved.

Even More Penguin Fun!

Your Club Penguin experience doesn't have to end when you log off of the game. There are lots of cool things you can do right from the Club Penguin website, clubpenguin.com. Click on the orange penguin, or the word "Community" to access these things to do:

Make Some Art: Click on "Activities" to print out coloring pages, and pages that show you how to draw penguins yourself. Then click on "Fan Art" to learn how to submit your original drawings to the Fan Art page, which showcases Club Penguin art drawn by kids. Or, just peruse the latest art submitted by fans!

Get a Laugh: Click on "Comics" to read Club Penguin comic strips you won't find anywhere else!

Penguin-ize Your Computer: Click on "Wallpaper" to download wallpaper for your computer featuring your favorite games, Captain Rockhopper, and more!

Penguin Pride: Do you have your own website or blog? Click on "Fan Banners" to download banners with the Club Penguin logo. Show the world that you love Club Penguin!

CLUB PENGUIN TIMES JOKES

How Do I Do That?

"Whenever I give a tour, penguins ask me all kinds of questions. If you have a question, asking a Tour Guide is a good way to get an answer. You could also ask a friendly-looking penguin for help, or write to Aunt Arctic in *The Club Penguin Times.*"

How Do I Pour Coffee? Or Play Guitar? Or Do All Those Other Cool Things I See Penguins Doing?

It's not as hard as you think. There's a simple formula for most special actions:

Special Item + Dance (or Wave) = Special Action

First, you need a special item. Some items that allow you to do special actions are given away for free at parties. Others can be bought in catalogs, if you have a membership. Once you buy the item, put it on. Don't wear anything else. Then dance or wave to set the special action in motion.

Here are a few examples of how the special formula works. Of course, the best way to find out how to do a special action is to experiment and see what works!

Electric guitar + Dance = play guitar
Hawaiian skirt + Dance = do the hula
Propeller cap + Dance = hover
Whistle + Wave = blow whistle

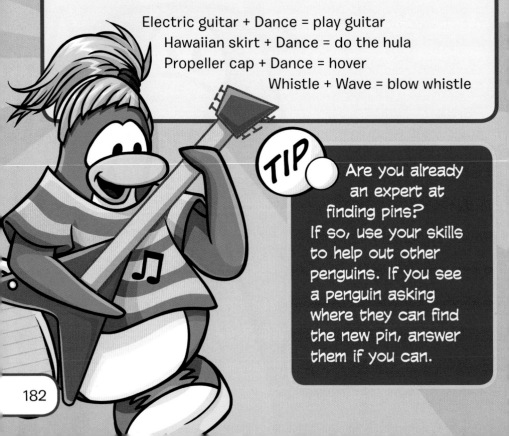

TIP

Are you already an expert at finding pins? If so, use your skills to help out other penguins. If you see a penguin asking where they can find the new pin, answer them if you can.

How Do I Find the Hidden Pins?

Every two weeks, a new pin is hidden in Club Penguin. A pin is a small picture that you can add to your player card. To learn when a new pin is out, check the last page of the newspaper.

Searching for a pin is fun. Check all over Club Penguin, and look for a small icon that doesn't belong. Sometimes you need to take special action to find a pin. During the Winter Fiesta of 2007, for example, you had to move your mouse over a piñata to break it open. Then the hidden pin fell out!

There are two things you should know when searching for pins: A pin is never hidden in Town Center, because it is too crowded there. And a pin will never be hidden in the same place two times in a row.

Cool Pins!

There have been more than fifty pins released since Club Penguin opened in 2005. Here is a sampling of them:

 candy cane   anchor

 pot of gold   surfboard

 teddy bear   UFO

 jellyfish   ruby

 cactus   camping tent

All About You

"This tour might be over, but you can have new adventures in Club Penguin every day. Take this fun quiz, then use the pages in this section to keep a record of your experience."

Quiz: What Kind of Penguin Are You?

Do you consider yourself a bookworm? A sports fanatic? The life of the party? Even if you think you know what kind of penguin you are, take this quiz to see if you're right. The answer may surprise you!

Pick the best answer to each question. Then add up the points you get for each answer. Use the chart at the end to learn your penguin identity.

1. What is your favorite way to spend a Saturday afternoon?
   a. Going sledding (5 pts.)
   b. Going to an outdoor fair (4 pts.)
   c. Volunteering at the Tour Guide booth (3 pts.)
   d. Playing *Thin Ice* (2 pts.)
   e. Reading in the Book Room (1 pt.)

2. Where is your favorite place to visit?
   a. The Cove (5 pts.)
   b. The Night Club (4 pts.)
   c. I don't care where I go, as long as I'm with my friends. (3 pts.)
   d. The Dance Lounge (2 pts.)
   e. Your igloo (1 pt.)

3. Where is your favorite place to grab a bite?

    a. I like to play *Ice Fishing* and catch my own fish. (5 pts.)

    b. Who needs to eat? Let's dance! (4 pts.)

    c. I like to hang out at the Coffee Shop with my friends. (3 pts.)

    d. I like to grab a quick slice of pizza; it's easy to eat while playing video games. (2 pts.)

    e. I like to cook on the grill in my igloo. (1 pt.)

4. What do you like to wear when you go out?

    a. A football jersey or other sports gear (5 pts.)

    b. Whatever is brand-new in the Penguin Style catalog! (4 pts.)

    c. My friends and I try to dress alike. (3 pts.)

    d. I don't really care what I wear. (2 pts.)

    e. I don't go out. (1 pt.)

5. What is your favorite season of the year, and why?

    a. Winter, because that's ice hockey season! (5 pts.)

    b. I like them all, because there is always a new party every month. (4 pts.)

    c. Summer, because I get to spend more time with my friends. (3 pts.)

    d. It doesn't matter, because I like to stay inside and play games. (2 pts.)

    e. I like them all, because I am comfortable in my home all year long. (1 pt.)

Add Up Your Score:

22-25 points: You are an adventurous penguin who loves being outdoors and enjoys competitive sports and anything extreme.
Colors to try: Red, bright blue
Activities to try: *Jet Pack Adventure*, *Sled Racing*, *Cart Surfer*, swimming at the Cove

18-21 points: You are a party-loving penguin who loves to dance the night away! All you need is music and a dance floor to be happy.
Colors to try: Lime green, orange, bright pink
Activities to try: Igloo parties on the map or dancing in the Night Club

13-17 points: You are a social penguin who loves to be with your friends and help when you're needed. You really don't like being alone.
Colors to try: Yellow, green
Activities to try: Become a Tour Guide, put on a play at The Stage, or start a snowball fight at the Snow Forts

9-12 points: You are a penguin who loves to play video games! You may discover you'll get the same rush challenging another penguin to a one-on-one board game.
Colors to try: Black, red, purple
Activities to try: *Thin Ice*, *Astro Barrier*, *mancala*, *Find Four*

5-8 points: You are a real homebody who doesn't like crowds. You might find you enjoy some of Club Penguin's quieter spots.
Colors to try: Brown, dark green
Activities to try: Try venturing out of your igloo once in a while! Go to the Forest and breathe the fresh air. Read a book in the Book Room. Or invite a buddy over for a two-person party.

The Basics

My penguin's name: _____

Favorite penguin color: _____

My puffles: _____

Name   Color

_____   _____
_____   _____
_____   _____
_____   _____
_____   _____
_____   _____
_____   _____
_____   _____

My best buddies:

_____
_____
_____
_____
_____
_____
_____
_____

Favorites

Favorite game: _____

Favorite hangout: _____

Favorite party spot: _____

Favorite clothing item: _____

Favorite furniture item: _____

Favorite book in the Library: _____

Favorite Club Penguin character: _____

Favorite Club Penguin party: _____

Favorite pizza: _____

Highest Game Scores

Aqua Grabber

Score: _____ Date: _____

Score: _____ Date: _____

Score: _____ Date: _____

Astro-Barrier

Score: _____ Date: _____

Score: _____ Date: _____

Score: _____ Date: _____

Bean Counters

Score: _____ Date: _____

Score: _____ Date: _____

Score: _____ Date: _____

Cart Surfing

Score: _____ Date: _____

Score: _____ Date: _____

Score: _____ Date: _____

Catchin' Waves

Score: _____ Date: _____

Score: _____ Date: _____

Score: _____ Date: _____

Hydro-Hopper

Score: _____   Date: _____

Score: _____   Date: _____

Score: _____   Date: _____

Ice Fishing

Score: _____   Date: _____

Score: _____   Date: _____

Score: _____   Date: _____

Jet Pack Adventure

Score: _____   Date: _____

Score: _____   Date: _____

Score: _____   Date: _____

Pizzatron 3000

Score: _____   Date: _____

Score: _____   Date: _____

Score: _____   Date: _____

Puffle Round-Up

Score: _____   Date: _____

Score: _____   Date: _____

Score: _____   Date: _____

Thin Ice

Score: _____   Date: _____

Score: _____   Date: _____

Score: _____   Date: _____

Free Items

Item: _____ Date: _____

Item: _____ Date: _____

Item: _____ Date: _____

Item: _____ Date: _____

Item: _____ Date: _____

Item: _____ Date: _____

Item: _____ Date: _____

Item: _____ Date: _____

Item: _____ Date: _____

Item: _____ Date: _____

Item: _____ Date: _____

Item: _____ Date: _____

Item: _____ Date: _____

Item: _____ Date: _____

Item: _____ Date: _____

Item: _____ Date: _____